ROOFING RIPOFF

Why Your Asphalt Shingles Are Failing and What You Can Do About It

by Tim Carter

Nationally Syndicated Columnist
and
Founder of AsktheBuilder.com

ROOFING RIPOFF
Why Your Asphalt Shingles Are Failing
and What You Can Do About It

Copyright ©2017 by Tim Carter

ISBN-13: 978-0-9989709-0-5
ISBN-10: 0-9989709-0-5

Cover design by Mary Beth Wilker
www.wilkerdesign.com

Interior Design by SheridanINK
www.sheridanINK.com

www.askthebuilder.com

First Edition

Printed in the U.S.A

ACKNOWLEDGEMENTS

It's important for you to realize this book was made possible by hundreds of people who have helped me along my journey. Many have contributed to the effort and their input, support, and tips over the years provided the fuel to keep me going.

It's impossible for me to name them all and I apologize now if I don't give you the accolades you deserve.

First and foremost is my dear wife Kathy. Her unconditional love, unending patience and support through all our years together created the strong foundation this book is built upon. Thank you so much Kathy!

My three children, Meghan, Tristan and Kelly contributed unknowingly by not complaining too much when I insisted on working down in my office rather than playing with them.

I want to thank Meghan especially for her guidance with the title of this book. I was, as usual, headed down the wrong path.

While I've already sent my mom and dad back to Heaven, I'm deeply indebted to them for bringing me into this world and allowing me to have my own room at the age of ten that had its own door to the outside world. All those late-night missions I successfully completed helped get me up on the life learning curve that much faster.

My sister Lynn has also helped with her support during the transition I made from full-time builder to full-time journalist.

Kathy's father and mother, Dan and Mary Jane Whalen, were instrumental in launching me down the building and remodeling pathway. When no bank would lend Kathy and I the money to buy our first vacant house with the large hole in the roof, they stepped in at the last moment to fund the venture. When we handed them the last check to repay the loan, I'm sure they were as proud as

Kathy and I were.

Ellen Rausch was the first employee at AsktheBuilder.com. Her endless energy and tolerance of my personality knows no bounds.

Roger Henthorn is also part of the www.AsktheBuilder.com team. Our friendship dates back to long before www.AsktheBuilder.com was even a glimmer in my eye. He's invested hundreds of hours helping me understand computers and making sure you get all the information you need when you visit www.AsktheBuilder.com.

Richard and Linda Anderson provided the first dollar of income for my new Ask the Builder career. Their check sits framed and behind glass and is one of my prized possessions. Their support through the years was instrumental in propping me up when challenges seemed insurmountable.

Marty Hovey, Leo Notenboom and Steve Loyola have all helped along the way. These three friends have provided countless hours of graphics and deep-based server and technical support so www.AsktheBuilder.com can continue to say it's the oldest and longest lasting first-person home improvement website on the Internet.

Mary Beth Wilker took the rough sketch I created for the book cover after seeing it in a dream and created the grand finished product. She and her husband Nick Motz are dear friends of mine.

Ken Middleton bought overpriced ads on my fledgling radio program at 1450 WMOH allowing me launch my media career.

Charlie Murdock taught me how to use the word you.

Mark Ossege placed enormous trust in me allowing me to build my first custom home.

Larry Eisinger was the father of the modern DIY movement. He was a fellow syndicated columnist and provided invaluable insight into the newspaper and book publishing industry.

Brent Walter is now my son-in-law, but before that he helped tweak the www.AsktheBuilder.com website to enhance your experience once there.

Dave Weiner showed me how to think big and made my short-lived nationally syndicated radio show possible.

Jeff Walker shared so very much, not the least of which is the power of a subscriber list and the magic of psychology.

Dan Murray has been an inspiration for over a decade on and off the golf course and his generosity in tough times helped Kathy and I when we needed it the most. I'll be forever grateful.

Chuck Eglinton is a brilliant man who over the years has provided me with sage advice teaching me that if I want to keep your attention it's my job to make sure something is in it for you.

Countless www.AsktheBuilder.com newsletter subscribers have helped by just opening, reading and clicking the crazy links I put in the newsletter each week.

Jim Cluett is a new friend that showed me how to remove the negativity out of my daily life. This has allowed me to recapture wasted energy so I can enjoy my family and friends more and focus on projects like this book.

I'm indebted to Sheridan Stancliff for her skills and magic to make the printed version of this book look exactly how I wanted it.

Jack Greiner did his best to keep me safe from all those who will read this book and might feel I'm spreading scandalous speculation.

Thanks again to you if you're one that's helped me along the way.

TC

THE PLUMB BOB

A plumb bob is a simple tool that delivers extreme accuracy when it's used properly. Using one of the simple laws of physics, a plumb bob is drawn to the center of the Earth. When it's not moving, the line supporting the cone-shaped machined brass is perfectly plumb.

Newer technology incorporating laser light is trying to push the plumb bob out of favor, but a plumb bob needs no batteries to power it as does the laser. I've incorporated the two technologies in my logo because a laser line is also highly accurate.

I chose this basic tool as the symbol of my publishing company, Plumb Bob Press, because I strive to deliver to you reliable and accurate information.

When you see the small laser plumb bob at the bottom of each page in this book, it's your assurance the information you see is trustworthy.

Tim Carter
Publisher

TABLE OF CONTENTS

PROLOGUE

You and I are going on a journey.

We're going to discover why your asphalt shingle roof is disintegrating right before your eyes.

You see your gutters filling with the colored granules or collecting at the base of your downspouts.

Your shingles are curling like the fingers of an elderly person with arthritis.

Pieces of your roof are scattered in your yard after each moderate windstorm.

Hailstorms with small diameter hail inflict damage that years ago would have left your roof unscathed.

Your roof may have ugly black stains or streaks.

What you're about to read is a story of an industry that I feel might have lost its way.

That can happen when you travel, but it's not going to happen to us.

You won't be gone for long and I can assure you that as we make progress on our adventure you're going to experience a range of emotions ranging from shock to awe to anger.

Be brave.

Let's get going.

CHAPTER ONE
OUR SHARED PAIN

Remember just a few years ago when the roofer drove away and you relaxed under your new asphalt shingle roof?

My guess is you had a mixture of satisfaction, comfort and pride knowing you invested your hard-earned money wisely. Your new roof would look good and your home and possessions would stay dry for at least twenty, twenty-five, or more years until you sold your home.

That's what the warranty on the shingle brochure and the documents your roofer gave you at the end of the job said, right?

Life was good. You could now divert your attention, time and money to other pursuits.

Fast forward just ten years or so and my guess is you're one of the many homeowners that's dismayed, frustrated and furious because your asphalt shingle roof is falling apart.

Odds are you'll now have to spend thousands of dollars to replace your roof long before its time.

Here's how you'd know if your roof is in bad shape. Are your shingles

experiencing one, or more, of these defects long before the warranty is up:
- excessive loss of the colored ceramic granules
- curling edges
- cupping
- cracking
- brittleness
- ugly black streaks or stains

Here's but one example of what I'm talking about.

These are my own failed asphalt shingles on my New Hampshire home. These exact shingles looked perfect in the spring of 2008, but they started to fail soon after. This photo was taken late spring 2015 and the shingles were only 15 years into their projected 30-year lifespan.

You're not alone, as my own asphalt shingle roof, on my current home in New Hampshire, started to fail just nine years into its thirty-year-guaranteed life span.

Three years after I first noticed deterioration, the entire roof suffered a catastrophic failure over a harsh winter that left the shingles delaminating as the snow and ice melted.

Does this mean all asphalt roofing shingles are defective?

No.

I believe the facts I've discovered about asphalt shingles, my own personal

This roof was on the vacant Tilton, New Hampshire post office building. Note how most shingles are missing all the colored granules and the shingles are curled at the edges.

experience with these products over forty years, a fascinating look back at asphalt products that were made over eighty years ago, and hundreds of survey responses I've received from homeowners just like you will prove beyond a reasonable doubt that some shingle products in the marketplace appear to be sub-standard.

I suggest you and I go on a short journey even though you're busy with life. Yes, dealing with your failing asphalt shingles is no fun and you just want the pain to go away. I'm sure all you really want is an affordable roofing product that will perform as promised.

Start putting what you'll need in your backpack so we can get going. While you're getting ready, allow me to share with you why it's important for us to complete the trek.

LEGENDS AND MYTHS

When I was a young adult I read a fascinating and captivating book by J.R.R. Tolkien - *Lord of the Rings*.

In that book, Tolkien wrote, "*And some things that should not have been forgotten were lost. History became legend. Legend became myth. And for two and a half thousand years, the ring passed out of all knowledge.*"

That's a profound passage.

Tolkien verbalized what can happen to events, people and things that flow down the river of time and are lost to current and future generations.

Cloudy Family History

I'm sure you can relate to this. Perhaps there are mystical stories in your own family about a grandparent, or great grandparent, that did this or that, yet there's no photographs, nor statements by credible witnesses that validate the stories.

All that remains is hearsay. The stories just live in your memory and that of other family members or friends. All you can do is talk about them and people hear what you say.

Over time, as you know, the stories can change. Important facts can be left out or the stories can be embellished.

In many cases they can be forgotten.

Disappearing Old Roofers

What does this have to do with your asphalt shingle roof that looks like it's been on your home for fifty or more years?

It's easy.

There are only a few of us left that remember how asphalt shingles **used to perform**.

In other words, as more and more older builders, roofers and remodelers retire and die, their memories of what they saw up on roofs, what asphalt shingles looked like on a steep or low-slope roof after twenty-five, thirty-five and even forty years go with them to the grave.

The asphalt shingles themselves get buried deep in a landfill, making it difficult to do a scientific analysis of what was, or was not, in them. It makes it difficult to weigh them to see how they compare with shingles being made today.

Some shingles are being recycled now and become roadways that you and I drive upon. This is a great use of the material, but once they're put in the grinder, we're not able to test them.

CURATING MY MEMORIES & EXPERIENCE

I'm not going to allow my crisp and vivid memories to disappear and pass out of all knowledge. That's part of my motivation for writing this book.

But the primary inspiration for writing this book lies in the fact that when the roof on my own home failed at such a rapid and alarming pace and I switched hats from simple homeowner like you to nationally syndicated newspaper columnist and was rebuffed by the major players in the asphalt shingle industry, I suspected something was amiss.

For the past twenty-three years I've built my Ask the Builder brand by doing my best to discover the truth about products via my weekly column.

I decided to approach the defective asphalt shingles subject as an investigation and went looking for answers from some of the giant asphalt roofing manufacturers you'd recognize and the industry association that represents them.

Guess what?

They refused to answer my pointed questions. As work progressed to complete this book, they continued to ignore my emails and several social media requests.

Do you want to know what I asked them? I thought so.

But before you read those questions, let's go a little further down the pathway on our adventure so the questions make sense to you.

I hope you left some room in your backpack because along the way I want you to store some very important facts concerning asphalt shingles.

CHAPTER TWO
MY BASE KNOWLEDGE

Building, remodeling and writing are part of my core DNA.

At an early age, I used to try to fix things around my mom and dad's home. I got the home repairs merit badge in Boy Scouts.

I was the editor of my high school newspaper. In college my friend John Pendery and I worked on the weekends and in the summer as laborers for a man that purchased old run-down homes and restored them.

As soon as I graduated from college, I started my own home remodeling and repair business.

I was fortunate to live in Cincinnati, Ohio where there was an abundance of homes that had a wide variety of roofing materials.

Thousands of homes had real slate roofing. Many older homes had tin-plated steel roofs or portions of the roof covered with this marvelous material. A few homes had wood cedar shakes. Some roofs were covered by thin sheets of cement reinforced with asbestos.

But the vast majority of homes had asphalt shingles and they still have a stranglehold on the market today.

If you visit the Asphalt Roofing Manufacturers Association website, they say that "*.... asphalt shingles can be found atop more than 80 percent of American homes...*"

Asphalt shingles have traditionally been the mainstay here in the USA for the past 100 years because they're cheaper to make and install than just about any other roofing material.

MY MEMORIES

Remember what I said about memories? Here are mine about asphalt shingles that I saw, installed and had on my own home.

In all my years of working on older homes that had asphalt shingles, I never recall ever seeing the issues like I'm seeing, and other homeowners like you are experiencing, today.

Sure, there was an occasional worn-out and neglected asphalt shingle roof that was still in service. The owner of the building either didn't have the money or didn't care to replace his failing roof.

It was not uncommon just thirty or forty years ago for standard asphalt shingles to outlast the warranty.

THE THREE-TAB SHINGLE

When I first got into the construction business in the autumn of 1974, the primary asphalt shingle was the three-tab shingle. You can still purchase them today.

Each white tab is just under 12-inches wide and the tabs are 5-inches high. The wider black strip above the tabs will be covered by the next row of shingles. If you use these shingles on a roof, all you'll see are the white tabs once all the shingles are installed.

These traditional shingles came with a standard fifteen-year warranty. It was not uncommon for them to last twenty or twenty-five years.

This is a standard three-tab shingle. These are still available and used on many homes.

I can't ever recall seeing a roof lose many of its colored ceramic granules seven years into their life.

Would you believe me if I told you that some homes in older neighborhoods with lots of shade trees had standard asphalt shingles that could last thirty and even forty years and still look good?

Well, it's true.

My Own Queen Anne Victorian Asphalt Roof

I've installed thousands and thousands of asphalt shingles with my bare hands over the past forty years.

One of the roofs that was near and dear to my heart was the stunning Queen Anne Victorian home I built for my wife back in 1986 in Amberley Village, Ohio. Amberley Village is a small town that's part of greater Cincinnati, Ohio.

We moved into our new home the summer of 1987 and moved out in 2010 when we relocated to New Hampshire. We purchased our New Hampshire home in 2008 and I traveled back and forth between the two houses over a twenty-two month period.

Back thirty years ago I couldn't afford the roof that Cincinnati house deserved so I had to roof it with the plain-vanilla three-tab asphalt shingle.

By this time, fiberglass shingles were the rage of the USA marketplace. Just about every asphalt shingle manufacturer had switched over to fiberglass as the base mat instead of the organic paper mat they had used for decades.

That simple three-tab shingle made by one of the biggest and most recognized manufacturers in the marketplace came with just a fifteen-year warranty. That means if it lasted fifteen years, I'd be happy that I got my money's worth.

But it didn't last fifteen years. It lasted much longer and I believe it could still be protecting the home and all that's inside it.

You can see this actual roof in a video I taped in 2006. The roof was twenty-years old at this point. The section of the roof you see faced southeast and received brutal sunlight from just after sunrise each day until mid-afternoon.

You can see the roof shingles exhibit no granule loss, they're not curled and they still have enough flexibility in them to allow me to install a bath fan vent flashing twenty years later without cracking the shingles!

Go here to watch the video: http://go.askthebuilder.com/amberleyroof

Replace for Resale

I replaced the roof in 2009 not because it was in poor shape, but because I was selling the home the following year and knew that a home inspector would state in his report the roof had outlived its warranty by ten years!

Think about that. In 2009 there were no spots at all where colored granules were missing. The shingles were not cupping or curling. The self-adhesive material under each tab was still working and the shingles were glued to one another.

My guess is the roof had still another ten years of life and it's possible it could have lasted until 2025!

The New Normal

This was normal back just fifteen or twenty years ago. You simply didn't see disintegrating asphalt shingle roofs like you do today.

As I write these words, I'm reflecting on what was once a robust product now appears to be one that's disposable. The good news is I believe I've discovered at least two asphalt shingle products that have the pedigree of a product first manufactured nearly one hundred years ago!

Furthermore, I've discovered a way to extend the useful life of asphalt shingles so they perform just like the shingles I used to work with all those years ago.

But before you and I talk about those, allow me to share the details of my own roof and other things that should be of great interest to you about asphalt shingles.

CHAPTER THREE
MY FAILED ROOF

This book would have never been written had it not been for my own asphalt shingle roof falling apart within years after moving into my home in New Hampshire.

I didn't build the home I'm living in and the builder who constructed it installed a shingle that came with a thirty-year warranty. The house was built around the year 2000. When I looked at the roof the spring of 2008 while seeing the home with my realtor, the roof looked brand new.

I thought to myself I might never have to replace the roof in my lifetime.

Sadly I was wrong.

FIRST SIGNS OF TROUBLE

Many homes in New Hampshire don't have gutters because the snow and ice buildups tend to rip them off homes as the ice and snow slide off the roofs.

I decided to install gutters at several locations around my home to stop water from splashing up against the front door and rear doors on the deck. I did this the summer of 2009.

Shortly after doing this I noticed a significant amount of colored mineral granules collecting in the gutters. I knew this shouldn't be happening with an asphalt shingle roof that was not yet ten years old.

It's quite possible this granule loss was happening before the gutters were installed and it was hard to notice. The granules would have fallen onto the ground and through the cracks of my rear deck. The first fall after installing the gutters I scooped out handfuls of colored granules along with the leaves.

MORE GRANULES & CURLING

Fast forward a few years to the year 2012. Just above my front door there are three roofs that connect. In the two valleys where the roof sections touch, the shingles started to show excessive wear and deterioration.

There were patches where all the colored granules were missing and the shingles were beginning to curl. I knew then the roof was in a serious state of decline and started to pay very close attention to it.

THE WINTER OF 2014-2015

Winters in New Hampshire can be harsh, very harsh. The winter of 2014-2015 was no exception. As the winter progressed, I noticed an alarming issue where my architectural shingles started to delaminate.

My shingles were made using two different strips of shingle material. The lower layer was a solid sheet about 7 inches tall. The top layer was about 13 inches tall and a little over 36 inches wide.

The top layer had rectangular cutouts that created a three-dimensional look resembling wood shakes. This type of shingle had been around since the 1980s and was considered better looking than the standard three-tab shingle.

My house roof has a steep 12 / 12-pitch roof and gravity finally won the battle as the asphalt cement used to bond the lower layer to the upper layer of some of the shingles lost its adhesive power.

The lower layer of some shingles detached completely and slid to the ground. In other cases they slid out and hung at an angle. When I picked up those that fell they were extremely brittle and crumbled with little effort.

This is not how I remembered a ten or twelve-year-old shingle to be. I prayed the roof would last until the summer when I could replace it.

The Hot Summer of 2015

I started to replace my roof the day after Memorial Day, 2015. It was a blistering hot day for New Hampshire. Little did I know but Mother Nature had decided she was going to serve up quite a few of these searing days as the summer season progressed.

As I began to strip the old asphalt shingles off I was stunned by how brittle they were. Never before in my career had I seen shingles fall apart in my hands as these.

The more shingles that I took off, the more my mood changed from concerned to angry. It's possible you share the same exact emotion as I had.

I was furious that I was sweating up on my roof replacing a roof that should not have been replaced for a minimum of fifteen more years, possibly twenty. After all, the warranty was for thirty years so the manufacturer surely felt the product would last for thirty years.

The Newspaper Ad

Just before starting the re-roofing job I noticed an ad in our local newspaper, *The Weirs Times*. This ad was purchased by a local roofing company and it talked about how they did roof inspections for failing asphalt shingle roofs. The ad also mentioned they helped with the paperwork to file a warranty claim.

I decided to call the owner of the roofing company and talk with him. When we connected, he mentioned that he was seeing asphalt shingle roofs fail all around the Lakes Region of New Hampshire. I live right in the center of this region.

When I asked him about the warranty claim for my roof, he chuckled saying it was pretty much a waste of time because the manufacturer was very tough to deal with. What's more, he said the average homeowner only got back several hundred dollars after jumping through many hoops.

My takeaway was to keep tearing off shingles and not worry about the warranty.

These are dimensional shingles. Just about every shingle manufacture offers this design.

ONE VERY HOT DAY

As the days progressed, I was working one day in early June and became very aggravated about the entire situation. I still had lots of work to do and decided that something was very wrong. It was time to get to the bottom of it.

I'm very lucky. For the past twenty-three years I've been a member of the working press. Back in October of 1993 I started writing the newspaper column *Ask the Builder*. Within three months I had self-syndicated it into thirty newspapers.

Writing for a large audience like that allows one to open lots of doors. I discovered many years ago that industry associations love to talk with me in the hopes that I'd feature their products in one of my columns.

For example, I had worked with the Portland Cement Association, the California Redwood Association, the National Wood Flooring Association and many others in the past. Each and every time I'd contact them, they were more than willing to answer all my questions.

On this hot and humid day I decided it was time to take off my Australian outback wide-brimmed hat protecting me from the sun and put on my investigative syndicated newspaper columnist's hat to attempt to get to the bottom of my failed roof.

The Tough Questions

After taking a shower and eating dinner that day, I went up to my hot and stuffy office in the attic above my garage. There I sat down and wrote a list of probing questions I felt would help me start to understand what was causing my shingles to fail.

You may feel the questions were too tough. I knew as I was writing them some might venture into trade-secret areas of making shingles. I discovered many years ago it's best to ask questions like this as sometimes the refusal to answer tells you something.

If the questions are too sensitive, manufacturers in the past just politely would mention they couldn't reveal trade secrets.

I decided to submit these questions to the Asphalt Roofing Manufacturers Association (ARMA) hoping they'd satisfy my curiosity. This association represents just about every manufacturer of asphalt shingles sold in the USA.

When I submitted the following questions, I told ARMA the reason I was contacting them was my own roof was falling apart and I was trying to determine what might be the cause of my own shingle failure. I was not involved in any class-action lawsuit and I had not initiated any personal legal action against the manufacturer of my own shingles.

Here are the questions I submitted to ARMA:

1. What are the components of a modern asphalt shingle? Please list everything without divulging a trade secret. I assume the list might be, but not limited to: liquid asphalt, a base mat, powdered limestone or other filler, ceramic granules and ???

2. Are there any other additives added to the shingle that contribute to the adhesion characteristic that holds the ceramic granules to the shingle?

3. Asphalt is derived by refining crude oil. Is it fair to assume that since there are different grades of crude oil, that there are different grades of asphalt?

4. If there are different grades of asphalt used to manufacture shingles, what are they?

5. How do the different grades or types of asphalt differ from one another? What is different with respect to their chemical makeup?

6. Does the different chemistry of asphalt affect the adhesive properties of the product? How so?

7. What can go wrong during the manufacturing process that might contribute to shingle quality? I'm looking for simple things like temperature of liquid asphalt, quantity of asphalt, too much filler, introduction of impurities, etc. Whatever might cause a problem.

8. Is there an asphalt that will take longer to become brittle? If so, what is different about it than an asphalt that becomes brittle faster? I'm looking for specific chemical attributes.

9. Why does an asphalt shingle become brittle? With respect to the chemistry, does this asphalt lose, at a faster rate, medium-weight hydrocarbons than an asphalt that remains pliable for many more years?

10. What's different about the asphalt component of today's shingles vs. those made fifty years ago?

11. Is there LESS asphalt in shingles made today vs. those made prior to the introduction of fiberglass mats? I'm assuming that we're talking about an apples to apples comparison of a shingle type. Take the standard 3-tab as an example.

12. Is it true that powdered limestone or other rock or ??? was introduced to the shingle manufacturing process with fiberglass mats to get the shingles up to the minimum weight of 240 pounds +/- per square?

13. Was powdered stone, or some other component, added to shingles prior to the introduction of fiberglass mats?

14. Houses built prior to 1970 rarely had any soffit ventilation and minimal gable end ventilation. Millions of these houses exist in older cities in the USA. Prior to 1970 there weren't widespread shingle failures from poor ventilation or heat build up. Why? Why would shingles on those houses fail today, but not in the 1960s?

15. If too much filler, powdered limestone, etc. is added to the shingle, how does it affect the adhesive properties of the asphalt?

The Responses

On June 11, 2015 I heard back from the Communications Director of ARMA, Ron Gumucio.

He said, *"Thank you for reaching out to ARMA, however without the facts and proper research we cannot comment. I would suggest you reach out to the individual manufacturers instead. Sorry I can't be of more help."*

Four days later I received an email from the Executive Vice President of ARMA, Mr. Reed Hitchcock.

Mr. Hitchcock wrote, *"Ron Gumucio, ARMA's Communication Director, forwarded me your inquiry regarding Asphalt Shingle litigation. I apologize for the late response as I was out of the country last week.*

While we certainly wouldn't want bad information or speculation circulating in the trade press as you suggested in your initial communication, as a trade association it is simply inappropriate for ARMA to involve itself in a commercial dispute involving one or more of our member companies. This is not a choice, it is fact. Individual companies are involved in these disputes, and each takes their own approach to responding as they see fit. If representatives of companies that you have reached-out to have referred you to us to comment, I would suggest that you're probably not in touch with the right people at those companies.

We would be glad to assist in any technical discussion where we can add value, but this is unfortunately not one of those discussions.

Please let me know if you have any other questions on this matter. And I hope we can collaborate on something positive in the future!"

CONFUSION

As you might expect, I was slightly confused by Mr. Hitchcock's response. In my original email to ARMA I had shed light on the fact that I was having trouble with my own roof, wanted to find out why it was failing and that I intended to write about it in a future column or article on my website.

I wasn't involved in a dispute with the manufacturer of my asphalt shingle. I just wanted the association to shed some light on how shingles were made so I could understand the reason(s) for my shingle failure at such an early point in their projected lifespan.

I took a deep breath after reading Mr. Hitchcock's email response and decided to do exactly what he suggested.

It was time to reach out to one or more of the ARMA member companies.

CHAPTER FOUR
NO COMMENT

The ARMA's responses to my questions made me feel uncomfortable. My gut screamed to me that I was onto something

It was now time to go hunting. I was determined to find out all I could about asphalt shingles because I knew something had changed.

My memories were still too fresh about my own home in Cincinnati that had a great asphalt shingle roof that showed no signs of failure even though it was over twenty years old.

THE BIG THREE

As of March, 2017 the list of residential manufacturer members of ARMA is as follows:

- Atlas Roofing Corporation
- Building Products of Canada
- Certainteed Roofing / Certainteed Corporation
- GAF

- Henry Corporation
- IKO Production, Inc.
- Malarkey Roofing Products
- Owens Corning
- PABCO Roofing Products
- Polyglass USA, Inc.
- Siplast Incorporated
- TAMKO Building Products, Inc.
- W.R. Grace & Co.

Three names should jump out at you on that list. They did to me and based on my years in the construction business, the three probably make the vast majority of asphalt shingles that are put on residential homes in the USA.

They are:

- Certainteed Roofing / Certainteed Corporation
- GAF
- Owens Corning

I decided to submit my list of questions to each of them to see what they had to say.

Certainteed Roofing and GAF declined to answer them. Owens Corning came back with a prepared statement and document that didn't at all address each of my questions.

Never in my over two decades of asking questions to countless companies had I run into this.

Now, more than ever, I was determined to find out what was wrong with asphalt shingles.

But first I had to get my roof finished. Four more months would pass and each day while battling the heat I thought more and more about not getting answers to my list of questions.

All sorts of questions ran through my head as I would throw handfuls of my crumbling shingles up over the edge of the dumpster week after week as the summer progressed.

How widespread was the issue?

Was it just in New Hampshire?

Was it happening all over the USA?

When did it start?

What really changed in the shingles to make them wear out so fast?

Was it possible to locate shingles made thirty, or more, years ago to see how they compared to modern shingles?

Were there old asphalt shingle roofs out there that were still in fairly good shape?

Discovering the answers to these questions, and more, would have to wait until I nailed on the last cap shingle on my roof. That would happen in October, 2015.

When that day did arrive, I had a plan in place.

CHAPTER FIVE
ASPHALT PRODUCTS THAT LAST

As the summer of 2015 passed by and I would push the wheelbarrow towards the dumpster at the edge of my driveway, I'd look to the left at the narrow firewood

This is my own deluxe shed on the hill above my home. The snow is obscuring the low-cost thin dimensional shingles.

shelter I had built the year before. I'd then look up to the right on the hill at a large two-story shed I had built in the summer of 2012.

I did my best to match the roofs of both of these to my house roof. I installed a lower-cost green dimensional asphalt shingle to match what was on the house.

I clearly remember when applying the shingles to both structures that I was unimpressed by the weight of the shingles. They were considerably thinner than the asphalt shingles I remember installing years ago.

At the time I didn't think much of it, but I started to wonder if modern shingles were being made much lighter than the shingles of old.

THE SHINGLE-SIDED HOUSE

Every few days I'd have to drive to town for any number of reasons. On the way back home I'd always take a slightly different route.

The return trip took me past a small home that could be well over one hundred years old. Next to it is a small one-car detached garage.

Both the house and the garage are covered with a product that looks like asphalt shingles. I'd seen this product for the first time about fifty-five years ago because it covered the home of one of my grade-school classmates.

Although the siding on this house and garage was not on the roof, it was in extremely good condition for its age. If it had been made like the shingles on my own roof, I would have thought the siding would have failed many years before.

I've looked closely at this material on many different houses and buildings. Years ago it was made using the same materials the companies would put in asphalt shingles. If you examine a piece of this siding you'll see:

- colored ceramic-coated granules
- asphalt
- wood-fiber core

The only major difference I could see between this asphalt-based siding material and asphalt shingles was the thickness and shape of the material.

The siding products were often made using a thicker wood-fiber mat. The underside and top were saturated with the liquid asphalt and the colored granules were placed into the wet asphalt.

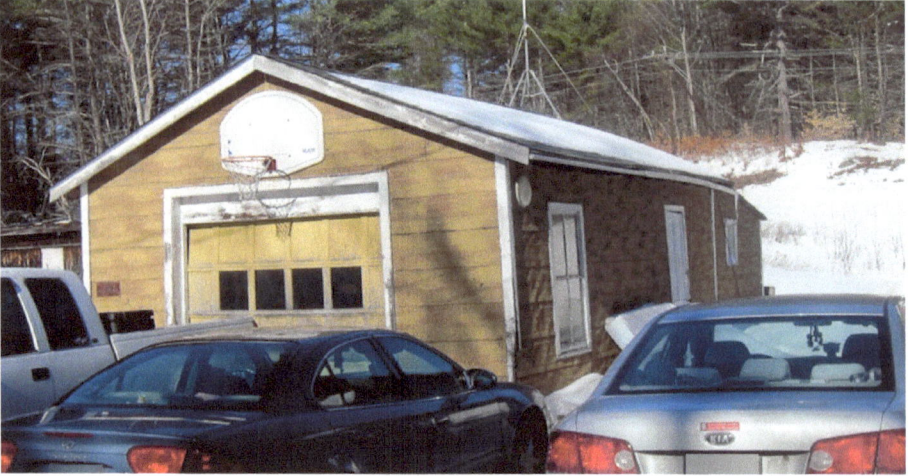

This is an old garage on Dow Road in Meredith, New Hampshire. It's covered with a siding that was made the same way shingles were made decades ago. The garage-door wall faces south and still looks great.

If you've ever had the opportunity to look at these older materials I think you'll find them intriguing because of the skill used by the manufactures to replicate the look of brick and stone. I wish I could go back in time and do a factory tour to see how the colored granules were placed so precisely on the panels.

You've probably seen this strange siding material on older buildings, but not given it a second thought. It was a very popular exterior siding material that was first applied to buildings in the early 1930s. The siding finally fell out of favor in the mid 1960s.

It was no doubt pushed aside by aluminum siding, a new and attractive alternative that took the residential remodeling market by storm.

I hadn't thought much about this house and garage before even though I had passed it hundreds of times in the past seven years.

But now I slowed down and looked closely at it each time I went by. I was stunned by how good the material looked after being exposed to the elements for decades.

The colored ceramic granules looked no different than what were on my roof and countless others. The asphalt used to saturate the wood fibers couldn't be that much different, could it?

How was it virtually none of the colored granules had come off, yet the granules on my shingles came off with each rainfall?

The gears in my head spun faster each day.

INSELBRIC

Perhaps the most popular brand of this unique siding product was called Inselbric. It was first used in the USA on October 15, 1931 as evidenced by their trademark application.

On the application the manufacturer described the product as "building

This is the house on Dow Road in Meredith, New Hampshire. The entire home is covered with a similar siding made just like asphalt shingles. It's possible this siding has been on the home since the mid 1930s.

covering materials in the form of asphalt impregnated or asphalt mastic or composition sheets or units."

The manufacturer made five different versions of this product, but I've only ever seen two of them with my own eyes. My guess is that the other three were not big sellers.

The five products were:

- 3D-INSELUM - Aluminum Insulating Siding
- INSELSTONE Insulating Siding
- INSELSYDE Plastic Insulating Siding
- INSELBRIC Insulating Siding
- INSELWOOD Insulating Siding

A small detached garage just a few miles from my home is covered with the INSELSTONE. Here's a photo of the small garage tucked into the woods. The longer wall faces east and the small wall faces north.

INSELBRIC IN NEWPORT, NH

One day in the fall of 2015 I traveled west from my home with a friend of mine.

This is the small one-car garage just miles from my home. It's covered with INSELSTONE. The east, west and north walls look perfect. The south-facing wall does have some colored granule loss.

We were going to meet another friend in Newport, NH for lunch.

As we turned into the parking lot of the pizza parlor, I looked at a tall older building just across the river from where I was.

The building was covered with Inselbric. The side I was looking at faced south and some of the sheets were falling off and there were patches where the colored granules had worn away.

It's impossible for me to know when this Inselbric was installed on this old building, but I feel it's safe to say it's been on for no less than fifty years, and quite possibly seventy or eighty years.

After placing my lunch order, I went outside to take photos. The east and north-facing sides of the building looked in perfect condition. You may find this hard to believe, but the siding looked brand new on the north side of the building.

This is a close up of the INSELSTONE siding. The detail achieved with the colored granules to create a three-dimensional look is remarkable. This siding is in excellent condition. It's possible it was installed before World War Two.

SOLAR DEGRADATION

It was obvious the sun was causing the siding to disintegrate. The south-facing siding was under assault any sunny day while the north-facing wall never got

This is the large building in Newport, New Hampshire covered with INSELBRIC. This wall faces due south and you can see much of it is still in excellent condition. They stopped making this siding in the 1960s, so this siding is at least fifty years old!

direct sunlight. The east-facing wall only got morning sun and as the sun climbed higher in the sky the ultraviolet (UV) rays just got in a glancing blow.

What's more, I knew from other research for other columns I've written in the past the early morning and late afternoon UV rays are rendered nearly powerless because they're passing through so much of the Earth's atmosphere.

As the sun is low in the sky its UV rays need to pass through many miles of the atmosphere. The higher the sun climbs in the sky, the less atmosphere its rays penetrate. This is why you and I get sunburned so quickly between 10 a.m. and 2 p.m.

I've known for years the power of the sun's UV light as I've written about how it destroys deck sealers, causes house paint to chalk, and breaks down fabric dye and fibers. Consider how UV light attacks the different parts of a deck.

If you have a wood deck, you no doubt have noticed the wood decking looks horrible while the sealer on the vertical parts of the deck railings almost always looks much much better. During the middle of the day, when the sun's UV rays are the most intense, they're just glancing off the vertical faces of the railing. But these same rays are hitting the decking at almost a 90-degree angle blasting apart the sealer molecules.

The sun's UV rays are more powerful than you might imagine and a few months later I'd discover just how powerful they really were.

Looking at the Inselbric on this building I also thought about how heat may be a contributing factor to the granules falling off. Heat had to be part of the issue, but to what extent?

No Disputing The Facts

All sorts of thoughts swirled through my head and I talked about it with my two friends as we ate lunch. Here's what I knew at this point to be true:

- My simple asphalt shingle roof on my Cincinnati, Ohio home was in excellent shape after twenty-plus years of service and much of it took the full force of the sun
- The Inselbric buildings I'd seen in New Hampshire were still in reasonable shape, some much better than others
- Countless roofs I'd worked on over the past forty years were also in great shape after twenty, thirty and sometimes forty years
- My New Hampshire home roof was crumbling and curling with just fifteen years of service

I knew instinctively it wasn't fair to compare the Inselbric to roof shingles because the Inselbric is exposed to the sun at a different angle than shingles. But some of what I saw, and it still is in service as I write these words, that faces south is in very good condition.

Think about that. Some of the Inselbric that faces south on the buildings might have been exposed to the weather for almost eighty years.

This should be of great interest to you as it was to me.

CHAPTER SIX
CASTING A WIDE NET

It was now time to see if other people in the USA, like you, were having the same premature shingle failure I was experiencing. This was easy to accomplish using the Internet.

I sat down one day and just typed "shingle lawsuit" into a few different search engines. The search results were littered with numerous class-action lawsuits against asphalt shingle companies.

Obviously I wasn't the only person suffering.

MY NEWSPAPER COLUMN

I decided in the fall of 2015 to leverage the platform I have with my syndicated newspaper column. I reached out to my syndicate editor and asked him if I could submit a column that deviated from my regular format.

I wanted to write about my failed shingle roof and then ask my readers in the different cities my column appears to contact me with their stories and photographs.

I had created a form on my AsktheBuilder.com website that a homeowner could fill out to tell me their story.

My editor thought it was a great idea.

Within weeks the floodgates opened and hundreds and hundreds of my readers all across the USA filled out the form. Quite a few sent in photos of their roofs that were falling apart long before the warranty had expired.

My Newsletter Subscribers

At the same time, I decided to reach out to my newsletter subscribers. I've published a newsletter since the late 1990s and the subscriber base was now up over 51,000. While I have subscribers from many nations across the world, I was only interested in responses from homeowners in the USA and Canada.

Once again, I received many many responses. The responses were proof the disintegrating shingle issue was widespread.

Some of the responses were painful to read. More than one homeowner had invested a considerable amount of their savings into their roof, and within a few years it was falling apart. They had no idea how they were going to pay for a replacement.

A Neighbor's Roof

One of my newsletter subscribers emailed me directly after seeing my request for stories. He lived west of me about thirty miles and I decided to go look at his roof.

It was in bad shape. He had solicited bids to get it replaced and the prices shocked him. He asked me for advice about what to do. He was not experiencing any leaks at this point and I knew his roof had a few more years of life in it.

His shingle defects were cosmetic with lots of curling shingles and significant ceramic granule loss. After talking with him, we discovered his roof and mine were made by the same company and manufactured probably within a year of each other. His house was built in 1999 and mine in 2000.

He was experiencing the exact type of failure as I saw on my own roof. His

These shingles were made by the same company that made my failed shingles. They are the same design but covered with black granules. They were sixteen years old when I took this photo in the fall of 2015. The warranty said they'd not start to go bad until the year 2029!

shingles had large areas of granule loss and curling. I took several photos and some video of his failing shingles. His understanding was they were supposed to last another fifteen years before they'd start to exhibit any visible defects.

RUSS'S ROOF

I have a friend who lives in Montrose, California. It's a small hamlet in southern California tucked up against the south flank of the San Gabriel Mountains. Look at the weather almanac for Los Angeles County and you'll discover my friend's roof gets sunlight on it an average of 283 days per year. That's seventy-seven percent of the year.

Russ grew up in the house he lives in. It's a stunning Craftsman-style home with a low-pitch roof. This means sunlight hits the shingles at about a 90-degree angle delivering the most powerful UV rays to the asphalt.

I was at his house in December, 2016 and I asked if I could climb around on the roof to look at it. Russ had told me it was time for a new roof and asked me to comment on anything he should know about.

Up on top of his home many of the shingles were falling apart. But the roof still was doing a great job of keeping Russ, his wife, and their possessions dry.

There were quite a few shingles that were missing the colored granules in places and there was some curling. I tested the shingles and they were quite brittle as I was able to break off the corners of a few of the shingle tabs. I took several photos of Russ's shingles paying attention to the ones that receive no shade at all during the day. The shingles on my friend's roof are exposed to sunlight from morning to night.

You can see that most of the shingles are laying flat and most of the tabs still have lots of the white ceramic colored granules.

These shingles were installed in 1965. That's fifty-one years ago from when I walked on them and took my photos.

How is it that Russ's shingles can last that long and my shingles, and maybe yours, couldn't make it but fifteen years looking far worse than his?

These are the shingles on my friend Russ's home in Montrose, California. They were installed in 1965.

HARD DATA DOESN'T LIE

Each week I was gathering more and more data. I still had lots more to collect.

One thing was certain. Manufacturers many years ago who made asphalt-based products for homesknew how to make products that looked very good after decades of exposure to the elements. The proof is undeniable.

Faced with this avalanche of data and a fair amount of heart-rending stories from my subscribers about financial hardship, it was now time to start to dig deeper.

I decided to jump feet first into researching exactly how shingles used to be made and what might have changed.

CHAPTER SEVEN
HISTORY OF ASPHALT SHINGLES

If you spend some time on the Internet and use the correct search terms, you'd be surprised what you discover. Different experts have published obscure articles and papers that go into great detail about how shingles used to be made.

One of the most interesting things I discovered was at the amazing website www.archive.org. There I stumbled across a fascinating book titled *Manufacture, Selection, and Application of Asphalt Roofing and Siding Products.*

It was the fourth edition and revised / published in January 1952. This tells you the book had been originally published some years before.

The Asphalt Roofing Industry Bureau was responsible for this fine book. This bureau eventually renamed itself as the Asphalt Roofing Manufacturers Association, the same association I approached with my list of questions.

All of what you're about to read can be verified by you doing what I did.

I believe it's advantageous for you to have an understanding of how asphalt shingles used to be made. A little later in the book I'll discuss how they're made today. While we're at it we'll explore the challenges shingle manufacturers have when working with asphalt.

Once you have this insight, you'll have your first clue as to why your colored shingle granules are leaving your roof faster than fans leaving a stadium as their favorite team is delivered a drubbing.

Birth Of An Industry

It all began in 1893 with the introduction of rolled asphalt roofing. By 1937 this young industry had already captured seventy-five percent of the roofing market in the USA. This grew to over eight-five percent by 1946.

The primary reasons for this explosive growth were four reasons:

- Fire resistance
- Appearance
- Ease of Installation
- Low Cost

By 1952, there were an astounding 145 asphalt shingle manufacturing plants spread out across the USA feeding the demand for the post World War II building boom.

Shingle Foundation

The foundation of an asphalt shingle used to be a roll of matting. This mat was made with cotton rags scraps that were obtained from clothing factories. Wood fiber and other cellulose was often added to create the mat.

But the composition of the mat started to change as clothing switched from cotton to man-made polyester fibers. The polyester didn't absorb the asphalt like the cotton did.

As the cotton rag market dwindled because less cotton was being used, shingle manufacturers migrated to a mat, or felt, that was a coarse paper derived from wood fibers.

The composition of the paper used to create the base mat for the shingles didn't change much for decades. This mat, as best as I can describe without seeing it, was a cross between a paper towel and a piece of cardboard. If you've ever seen a piece of cotton felt fabric, my guess is this paper product looked almost identical.

Strong & Absorbent

The mat needed to have enough tensile strength to be able to be pulled through the rollers at the shingle factory, yet be absorbent enough to soak up the liquid asphalt that provided the waterproofing quality needed so the paper mat would not rot once wet.

The industry referred to this paper as felt. If you know a little bit about roofing, I'm sure you've heard the term felt paper.

This paper came on very large rolls and was approximately one-sixteenth inch thick. If you look at a torn piece of cardboard you'll see the coarse fibers that you might see if you look at an older worn shingle that's lost its ceramic granules and the elements have stripped off the top asphalt coating.

The failed shingles on my own home appear to be made using this paper mat as I can clearly see what appear to be cellulose fibers using my 10X Hastings Triplet magnifier on some of the shingles I've saved.

I didn't submit my shingles to a testing lab to verify this, but I still have samples of my old shingles in my garage should someone want to test them.

Finally Fiberglass

The mat that's used by most manufacturers today is fiberglass. It's made from very fine interwoven fiberglass fibers. The reason the manufacturers switched from the paper-based mat to fiberglass will not surprise you, but we'll dive into that in a while.

Preserving the Paper

The trouble with paper is that once it gets wet, it will rot in a short amount of time. To preserve the paper felt mat, the manufacturers of old saturated it in liquid asphalt.

Asphalt is derived by refining crude oil. Asphalt is what's left over from crude oil after you remove from it other compounds like motor oil, jet fuel, diesel fuel, naphtha, paint thinner, gasoline and a myriad of other chemical compounds.

Asphalt is an amazing compound and does occur naturally in tar pits. It's a liquid, it's sticky and it's waterproof. That's why it's the perfect material to use for shingles. The manufacturers would heat this asphalt slightly so it was the consistency of hot maple syrup.

Historians have evidence that asphalt use stretches back about 5,000 years. It's an excellent natural preservative, it's got remarkable waterproofing characteristics, and it's quite sticky allowing you to glue things together.

To waterproof the paper felt mat, specifications decades ago called for saturating the mat with an amount of hot liquid asphalt that was 150 percent the weight of the paper. This just means for every pound of paper, you'd pour onto that section of paper 1.5 pounds of liquid asphalt.

This was the perfect amount of asphalt because it left the paper dry to the touch yet provided plenty of protection so water would not cause the paper mat to decay.

The asphalt used to protect the paper was called 'saturant'. It makes sense since it was used to *saturate* the paper to make it an effective water barrier. If you want to see what the shingle looked like at this stage of the process, all you need to do is hold a piece of 30-pound felt paper in your hand.

HARD CANDY

I have to believe you've had one or more M&M's®. Or perhaps you've had some Good & Plenty®. Both of these candies have a hard candy outer shell protecting a softer inner candy core.

That's the best analogy I can offer up to what the shingles of old resembled. The saturated felt paper represents the soft inner core of old shingles.

But the shingle manufacturers had to solve a problem many decades ago. They quickly discovered that the asphalt they used for the soft inner core would run down the roof under the force of gravity on a hot summer day. Something needed to be done to the asphalt so it would not liquify and flow down your roof.

Asphalt that comes to the roofing manufacturers from the oil refineries has a softening point that can range from 100 F to 150 F. The average is usually around 120 F. This is the temperature where the asphalt will start to flow down your roof to the gutters or the ground. This asphalt works fine to preserve the paper mat, but it can't be used to cover the outside of the mat in the next phase of manufacturing.

HOT ROOFS

The temperature of your asphalt shingle roof on a hot day in the summer can climb above 180 F. Your roof will experience temperatures like this the closer you are to the summer solstice when the sun is high in the sky going through the least amount of atmosphere.

On July 13, 2015 I took an infrared thermal photo of my own roof and recorded a temperature of 155.2 F. I did this with a FLIR thermal camera attached to a smart phone.

This is an infrared photo of my own roof. It's hard to see the temperature reading next to the white crosshairs, but the sensor said the shingles were 155.2 F.

Air Solved the Problem

Many decades ago the shingle manufacturers discovered if you heat up the asphalt to around 500 F and then bubble air through it, the liquid asphalt undergoes a magical chemical transformation.

Those deep in the asphalt shingle industry call this blow or blown asphalt, because they're 'blowing' air through the asphalt much like an artist who blows air into hot glass to form it or a child blows bubbles in a soda while waiting for food at a restaurant.

Oxygen in the air attaches to the asphalt molecules. The fancy name for this is oxidation. This oxygen promotes cross-linking of the asphalt molecules so they become bigger, larger and longer. This cross-linking has a detrimental effect in that it makes the asphalt stiff and brittle.

Just Enough Oxygen

It's important for asphalt to stay as supple as possible for as long as possible so it can hold onto the nice colored ceramic-coated granules you see down in your gutter that are supposed to be up on your shingles.

The manufacturers of old determined they could blow just enough air through the asphalt to raise the softening point from 120 F to around 200 F, or just above that, and still allow the asphalt to retain much of its flexibility. This is why the colored ceramic granules are still sticking to the sides of the Inselbric on the buildings I see here in New Hampshire and on my friend Russ's roof in California.

Keep in mind that the more oxygen you add to the hot asphalt the stiffer it becomes once it cools back down to normal temperatures.

Here's a clue: You can introduce oxygen to asphalt in two ways.

Coating the Felt

This oxidized asphalt that had the higher softening point of about 200 - 220 F was then used to coat both sides of the felt paper that was saturated with the unoxidized asphalt. This process made the shingles of old resemble the M&M's®

and Good & Plenty® you can eat today.

This simple two-part recipe is but one reason shingles from just a few decades ago lasted for much much longer than the shingles you probably have on your roof today.

It's very important for you to realize and remember that as you add more and more oxygen to the asphalt, it shortens its useful life up on your roof.

Natural Oxidation

The technique of stiffening the asphalt by adding oxygen happens on its own in nature, but at a far slower rate. Mother Nature can age asphalt all on her own.

The asphalt that does occur in nature in tar pits will stiffen and harden as it's exposed to the ultraviolet (UV) rays of the sun and air that contains oxygen. But this stiffening occurs over many decades under normal atmospheric conditions.

UV Attack

The UV rays of the sun that are blasting your shingles reach the asphalt in between the cracks where the ceramic-coated granules are, and any place where a granule might be missing.

UV light accelerates the oxidation of asphalt because it contains energy. Approximately five percent of the UV light is made up of energetic photons.

Think of these particles as tiny missiles. They hit the exposed asphalt and break molecular bonds creating a more-favorable environment for the asphalt to latch onto available oxygen in the air.

When these molecules are split they become chemically unstable. To get comfortable again, they'll grab oxygen from the air. The issue is the oxygen promotes cross-linking. Asphalt molecules up on your roof, and mine, can start to form long chains.

As long chains of asphalt molecules form, the asphalt becomes stiffer and stiffer losing its holding power. Granule loss starts to happen as the asphalt can't win the battle with gravity.

The last thing you want is to have the asphalt in your shingles exposed to direct sunlight. Once this happens, your shingles begin to degrade at an alarming rate, just as mine did.

Three years before I had to replace my own roof, it looked very good. Then the granules began to tumble to the ground faster than tumbleweeds skitter across the desert in a windstorm.

Each granule that tumbles off the roof exposes more asphalt to the sun. The UV rays begin an immediate assault. Any granules next to this exposed asphalt are now likely to become loose. It's a simple chain reaction.

ADVANCED AGING

Think of the best-used-by date you often see on food, drink and other products that have a shelf life. Asphalt that doesn't get heated and have oxygen bubbled into it has a much longer shelf life than asphalt that's subjected to accelerated oxidation at the asphalt shingle plant.

Many years ago the shingle manufacturers added just enough oxygen so the asphalt would not flow down your roof, but it would still have thirty, forty and maybe even fifty years of remaining life. I used to work with those shingles and had them on my own home.

Remember, as asphalt ages and becomes more oxidized, it becomes stiffer and stiffer and is unable to handle the back and forth expansion and contraction cycles that happen each time an asphalt shingle roof heats up from sunlight and then cools back down once the darkness of night envelopes your roof.

HEAT IS PART OF THE PROBLEM

Heat accelerates the oxidation process. You might have discovered this doing a simple experiment in high school chemistry class. This is why the shingles on the south and west facing portions of your roof look the worst if you happen to live in the Northern Hemisphere.

On my own home in New Hampshire, I had a small portion of roof that was shaded by a wall, it faced due north, and it never received direct sunlight. The shingles on that section of the roof were in much better condition than the shingles that received intense direct sunlight causing the temperature to soar above 150 F or more.

THE COLORED GRANULES

When the shingle stiffness gets to a certain point, the colored granules on the surface of the shingles begin to shed. These granules are not there for looks. They're the all-important sunscreen that protects the asphalt from UV attack which, as you now know, leads to oxidation. UV light supercharges the oxidation of the asphalt.

It should be obvious to you that shingle manufacturers have the ability to pre-age the asphalt in the shingles you buy. They do this via the amount of air that's bubbled into the black brew at the factory. Shingles can be made that only have a life expectancy of five, ten or just fifteen years.

If you add just a small amount of oxygen, the asphalt stays more flexible for a longer time. Add more oxygen and the shingles get stiffer in a shorter amount of time.

POWDERED LIMESTONE

Just about all asphalt shingles contain an ingredient to help make them firmer. Without this ingredient, the shingles would be very hard to work with in warm or hot weather. My guess is they'd be like working with a cooked wet fettuccine noodle.

As hard as I tried, I couldn't locate when powdered limestone was first used in asphalt shingles. My guess is many years ago because of how hard the shingles would be to work with in hot weather.I can tell you from personal experience that even with limestone in them, shingles on a hot day can be hard to handle and they can tear without too much trouble.

Powdered limestone is blended with the blown asphalt. This limestone, to a small degree, resembles the stones and sand you find in cast, or poured, concrete. Stones and sand in concrete are there to impart the strength of the finished hard concrete.

The limestone not only makes the shingles stronger, but it also allows the manufacturer to use less of the expensive asphalt.

Another benefit of the limestone is it helps build fire resistance since limestone doesn't burn and asphalt does.

Not Too Much

However, if you add too much limestone to the asphalt, you reduce the amount of sticky asphalt that's available to latch onto the all-important colored granules.

Furthermore, if you add too much limestone, it leads to black algae stains on shingles. Many years ago I have no recollection of black stains on asphalt shingle roofs.

To the best of my recollection, they just started to happen about the time the switch was made from paper mats to fiberglass.

The algae, *Gloeocapsa magma*, happens to love to eat limestone. If too much limestone is added to the shingles, it might be exposed at the surface of the asphalt and in the cracks between the colored granules.

Add water to the roof and the algae starts to grow. The black stains are the dark-

Multi-colored algae (red, black and green) are staining this roof just northwest of Newfound Lake in central New Hampshire.

colored cells of the algae. They don't hurt the shingles, but they look quite ugly. The good news is these stains do not cause any harm at all to the shingles. It's just an appearance issue much like you dripping ketchup on a clean shirt.

Later in the book I'm going to tell you how to get rid of these stains permanently.

But for now, it's time to share some fascinating data I uncovered about the actual manufacturing process when asphalt shingles are made. I believe you're going to find it quite interesting.

CHAPTER EIGHT
MAKING SHINGLES AND $ $ $

Let's go back in time about fifty or so years and look at what's happened in the asphalt shingle industry.

After World War II the US economy grew like wildfire. As more homes were built, it maxed out the manufacturing capacity of most asphalt shingle plants.

Because the plants were using paper felt as the base mat, you could only run the manufacturing line about 300 feet per minute. The tensile strength of the paper mat was the constraint.

If you tried to run the assembly line faster, the paper would tear. Companies that sold shingles to builders and roofing contractors often were on an allocation basis. The economic law of supply and demand was in play during this time period.

HIGH DEMAND = HIGHER PRICES

Because the demand was high and the supply was low or limited, asphalt shingle companies could charge a higher price for the product and reap higher profits.

For asphalt shingle companies to make even more money, they had to figure a way to make more shingles.

Here are just a few ways to achieve that:

- build more manufacturing plants
- run the factories 24 hours a day every day
- increase the speed of the existing manufacturing plants

The Fry Roofing Company chose to experiment with the third bullet point in the list back in the mid 1960s. They were the first company to substitute fiberglass for the paper used in the base mat.

Fiberglass was a game changer in many ways.

The first thing it did was allow the production capacity of a standard asphalt shingle plant to nearly triple. Instead of running the manufacturing line at 300 feet per minute, the speed increased to about 850 feet per minute.

This was possible because the fiberglass had a much greater tensile strength than the paper and was much more resistant to tearing when the rollers at the mill ran faster.

The manufacturers also discovered they no longer had to worry about protecting the fiberglass mat with the unoxidized asphalt. Since the fiberglass would not rot from getting wet, the manufacturers could just make one-step hard-candy asphalt shingles.

MORE MEANS LESS

There's a problem with increasing manufacturing capacity by a factor of 3X in a short amount of time. What was a shortage of shingles now became an oversupply.

In the 1970s prices of shingles started to fall with more plants switching from the organic paper mat to fiberglass. The fifty to sixty different asphalt manufacturers that existed back in the 1960s started to feel financial pressure.

Larger companies started to buy smaller companies in an effort to gain more market share. Owens Corning, for example, purchased the Lloyd A. Fry Roofing Company for $100 million cash. This was reported in the April 21, 1977 edition of the *Toledo Blade*. It was a natural as Owens Corning was one of the major producers of fiberglass.

Some companies went bankrupt because they simply couldn't compete.

To make money in the 1980s, those manufacturers still in business had to become more efficient.

As the industry moved from the 1980s into the 1990s, it started to lean more heavily on creative marketing. At this point, most companies had reached a plateau with respect to manufacturing efficiency.

To make more profit, you had to have a better mousetrap.

Now it was time to bring more styles and colors of shingles to the market. This razzle-dazzle was great eye candy for the consumer. Shingles that looked like wood shakes hit the market, laminated shingles were expanded to create deeper shadow lines, and shingles were created that simulated slate - one of the most durable roofing materials of all time.

WALL STREET BLUES

Today the fifty or sixty manufacturers have consolidated to about ten companies. A few of these companies are publicly traded.

I had the distinct pleasure years ago to be mentored about how to invest in stocks by a very astute CPA whose hobby was stock investing. As part of my training, he had me sit in on conference calls when he quizzed the top management of companies. He would ask very tough questions that related directly to increasing profits.

Can you imagine the types of questions savvy Wall Street analysts pose each quarter to the publicly traded asphalt shingle companies?

Can you imagine the pressure they put management under to meet or exceed earnings quarter after quarter?

If you were the president of an asphalt shingle manufacturer, what might you do to squeeze even more profit from the shingles you sell?

I've already given you a few clues and we'll get to that a little further down the trail. But for now, let's compare modern shingles with the shingles that were made just a few weeks before I graduated from high school in 1970.

CHAPTER NINE
OLD SHINGLES VS. NEW

Let's take a break on our journey and look at some new asphalt shingles right out of the pack. These are the same ones you can go out right now and buy in your city or town.

Don't you think it would be interesting to compare the actual shingle to the warranty offered for the shingle? You could also factor in price, but that's much harder to do because a particular product could be on sale or a promotion could be happening that gives you an artificially low price.

What's more, if you purchase a pallet or a minimum quantity, you can often get a cheaper price. I paid the highest price because I only purchased one bundle of each product.

For now, let's start with the thickness of some common shingles you might be able to buy today. Thickness is important because it's a measure of what separates your home from the wet weather outdoors.

I went to the local big box stores near my own home and purchased the top-of-the-line Owens Corning and GAF shingles with a lifetime warranty, and at the same time I picked up a bundle of shingles made by both manufacturers that come with their weakest warranties.

These were the only brands available at the two big box stores I visited. It's possible to visit lumberyards and other distributors to get other brands. GAF and Owens Corning are two of the giants in the asphalt shingle industry and I believe it's fair to say they manufacture a representative product.

I purchased:

- GAF Timberline ULTRA HD® (limited lifetime warranty)
- GAF Royal Sovereign® (25-year warranty)
- Owens Corning Duration® (limited lifetime warranty)
- Owens Corning Supreme® (25-year warranty)

I then got out my trusty Pittsburgh digital calipers that can take readings down to the hundredth of a millimeter. That's more than enough accuracy for measuring the gritty surface of an asphalt shingle.

DISCLAIMER: The actual shingle thickness can vary because of any number of factors. Here are just a few:

- size and orientation of the ceramic colored granules
- thickness differences in asphalt coating
- natural irregularities within the shingle

To get true scientific measurements, you'd have to measure lots of shingles from several packs, measure at different places across the shingles and then produce an average thickness. The size, shape and orientation of the colored ceramic granules can have a large impact on the thickness measurements.

I didn't go to that much trouble, but I did measure the thickness at several places on the shingles I examined.

Here are the average thickness measurements I recorded on the wear layer of each of the asphalt shingles:

GAF Timberline ULTRA HD®= 3.46 mm

GAF Royal Sovereign® = 2.78 mm

Owens Corning Duration® = 2.25 mm

Owens Corning Supreme® = 2.46 mm

No, that's not an error. The Owens Corning Duration shingle that has the limited lifetime warranty is thinner. That could mean it contains less material.

The GAF Timberline ULTRA HD® is thicker because they coat both sides of the shingle with the ceramic stone granules.

Here's what I paid for a bundle of each of the products:

GAF Timberline ULTRA HD® = $22.00

GAF Royal Sovereign® = $15.00

Owens Corning Duration® = $33.50

Owens Corning Supreme® = $29.00

Do The Math

If you get out your calculator you quickly discover something interesting. Let's look at the GAF shingles first.

The GAF Timberline ULTRA HD® shingle was only 0.68 mm thicker than the standard three-tab Royal Sovereign®. That means that the Timberline ULTRA HD® shingle is only 24 percent thicker than the bottom-of-the-line Royal Sovereign®.

But I paid 46.6 percent more for the Timberline ULTRA HD® shingle than the Royal Sovereign®. Remember, the pricing is a moving target because of so many different variables. However, you can see at first blush it doesn't make financial sense to purchase the Timberline shingle if you're not getting an equal amount of product for the extra money you're spending.

To be fair to GAF, you need to realize the Timberline ULTRA HD® shingle does have more product included. It's a laminated shingle design that has a dual layer of shingle over approximately 35 percent of the surface of the shingle.

It's vital for you to realize the common laminated shingle design does not provide you with any more protection from rain as once installed there are still parts of your roof that only have the same protection you'd receive from the basic three-tab shingle. Laminated shingles are simply an aesthetic treatment that attempts to make your roof appear as if it might be covered with wood shakes.

For this reason, that's why I feel it's fair to take price into consideration when comparing what you're getting at the end of the day. You want protection from the elements.

When you look at the Owens Corning example, the numbers just don't make sense to me. The more expensive shingle is thinner where it most counts and you're paying more money for it than their most-basic shingle.

That's very clever marketing if you ask me.

OLD UNUSED SHINGLES

Decades ago when I first got into the construction business back in the 1970s the industry standard for common three-tab shingles was a weight of 240 pounds per square.

A square is a unit of measure that's common in the roofing industry. For years

This is a scanned copy of J. Paul's actual receipt he got from the Philip Carey asphalt plant on May 21, 1970 when he arrived to put them in his truck. You can see the shingles used to weigh 240 pounds per square.

it's meant the quantity of material needed to cover 100 square feet of surface area with the finished roofing product.

I'm blessed to have a large and responsive newsletter subscriber base. I put out a call to my subscribers to see if anyone had old unused shingles stored in a garage, a shed or barn.

Four of my subscribers sent me old shingles that were just like the shingles I used to install. I now have these valuable historical samples stored safely in my garage.

The best ones were from J. Paul who lives in Harrison, OH. Not only did he have pristine leftover shingles that he purchased in 1970, but he also saved the original paperwork.

This paperwork clearly shows the shingles weighed 240 pounds a square or 3 pounds each because it takes 80 regular three-tab shingles to cover 100 square feet of surface area.

The order for the shingles was entered on May 19,1970. That date is circled in the upper left corner. He picked up the shingles from the Philip Carey loading dock in Lockland, Ohio on May 21, 1970. That date is written by hand in the Date Shipped box in the upper right corner of the receipt.

This is one of the original shingles J. Paul picked up on May 21, 1970. He mailed them to me while I was doing research for this book.

The third item on the ticket are the shingles. You can see there were 81 bundles with a total weight of 6,480 pounds. Divide 6,480 pounds by 81 and you get 80 pounds per bundle. It took three bundles of shingles to cover a square. Three times 80 pounds is 240 pounds.

I weighed the shingles that J. Paul sent me and all weighed just a few tenths of an ounce under three pounds.

You already know that's enough weight of material to provide a home with thirty years, or more, worth of protection. That's a very important data point.

WEIGHT OF MODERN SHINGLES

I decided it would be fascinating to weigh the new three-tab shingles I purchased as I wrote this book. I took random samples out of a bundle and determined an average weight.

To calculate the number of shingles you need to cover a square you just need to perform some simple grade school math.

The typical three-tab shingle today is still 36 inches wide. The shingle itself is about 12 inches high. The manner of installation requires that you overlap each row 7 inches on top of the row just below.

When you do this, each shingle has just 5 inches of its surface area exposed to the weather. Do the multiplication, 5 inches x 36 inches, and you should get 180 square inches of roof protection per shingle.

A square foot has 144 square inches. You achieve that by multiplying 12 inches by 12 inches. A square is 100 square feet so to arrive at the total square inches in a square, you just multiply 144 square inches by 100. That gives you 14,400 square inches in a square.

Divide 14,400 by 180 and you discover you need 80 standard three-tab shingles to cover a square. If we want the square of shingles to weigh 240 pounds, then each shingle must weigh three pounds (3 x 80=240).

SOMETHING IS MISSING

Now that we know what the simple three-tab shingle used to weigh, guess what the GAF Royal Sovereign® three-tab shingle weighed? I'm talking about the shingles I just purchased as I wrote this book.

Two pounds six ounces. If you put pencil to paper, you'll discover that's a total of just 190 pounds per square.

If you assume the granules weigh the same and there's the same amount of granules that can stick to the liquid asphalt when the shingles are made and the mat weighs just about the same, this means about 50 pounds of asphalt per square is missing from the shingles compared to those made just forty years ago.

GULP!

Guess what the Owens Corning Supreme® three-tab shingle weighed?

Two pounds five and one-half ounces. If my calculator batteries are good, that's a total of just 187.5 pounds per square.

I then weighed the Owens Corning Duration® shingle. This is a laminated shingle that's larger than a three-tab shingle. You need fewer shingles to cover 100 square feet.

The shingles are 39 and one-quarter inches wide and they're installed with 5.5 inches to the weather. Because a larger area of each shingle is exposed to the weather, you only need 67 shingles to cover a square.

The Duration shingle weighed in at three pounds three and one-half ounces. Sharpen your pencil and I'm quite certain you'll calculate that a square of these shingles weighs in at 215.7 pounds. Does this mean about 25 pounds of asphalt is missing?

A MARKETING TOOL

How can a shingle that weighs considerably less per square than the shingles of old have a much longer warranty? I understand it if the shingles have some new technology that's allowing them to last longer. But that doesn't seem to be what the data is telling us.

I believe if you look at all that's going on it's just another piece of evidence that the warranties speak more about the marketing than they do about the integrity and longevity of the product.

The GAF Timberline ULTRA HD® was by far the heaviest of the four shingles weighing in at a beefy four pounds fourteen ounces. However, don't think that the extra weight is in asphalt. As I said before, this shingle has the small ceramic granules on both sides of the shingle.

The GAF ULTRA HD® shingles, according to my math, weigh in at 326.6 pounds per square. But remember, the extra layer of stone could be what's in play here. It's pretty hard to measure the weight of the number of granules it takes to cover one side, so I'll leave that to your speculation.

EMOTIONS RUNNING HOT?

My guess is you might have a mixed and varied pot of alphabet-soup emotions starting to boil over by this time. You could be angry, perplexed, distraught, and feel helpless against the manufacturers who are offering to sell you their products.

You might have spent your life savings on a new roof recently or may have to take out a loan to replace a roof that should not have gone bad so soon.

I have a feeling that I may know what you're thinking.

"But Tim, what about the warranty that comes with the shingles? Won't that protect me?"

I believe you're going to be in for quite a shock.

CHAPTER TEN
WARRANTY EXPECTATIONS

Not too long ago I polled my newsletter subscribers asking them some questions about asphalt shingle performance and warranties. I wanted to get my head around what homeowners expected from their asphalt shingles.

My newsletter list is sent out to tens of thousands of consumers, most who live in the USA.

I was able to get 1,144 people to respond at the time I wrote these words. Each day more responses tumble in.

To be honest, I was somewhat surprised by a few of the answers. One thing that was very clear to me after studying the responses is that a large percentage of the homeowners I polled expect their shingles to look good and be leak-free for no less than twenty years. You'll see that question below and add up the percentages for 20, 25 and 25-plus years.

Here were the questions in the poll in the order in which they were asked:

Are you responsible, or share in the decisions, for the maintenance of the roof where you live? If the answer is "NO", there's no need for you to answer any other questions. Thanks.

98.4 percent responded Yes

I moved out of my parents' home in 1974. That was 43 years ago. Since then I've lived in one apartment and four houses. That means the average length of time I lived in one place after moving out was 8.6 years. Do the math and tell me what your average is after moving out of your parents' home.

47% said 12 or more years
13.2% said 5 or less years
7.9% said 8 years
7.7% said 10 years
7.7% sad 6 years
5.1% said 9 years
4.2% said 7 years
3.7% said 11 years
3.4% said they didn't know

When installing a new asphalt shingle roof or re-roofing your existing home, how many years do you expect the new asphalt shingle roof to look good AND be leakproof?

31.5% said 25-plus years
29.1% said 20 years
28.1% said 25 years
9.2% said 15 years
1.2% said 10 years
1% said they didn't know

If you're thinking of purchasing an asphalt shingle that claims it has a Limited Lifetime warranty, how many years do you expect it to last?

27.4% said 25 years
20.8% said 20 years
20% sad 35-plus years

17.1% said 30 years

6.8% said 15 years

2.5% said 10 years

5.4% said they didn't know

When you consider purchasing an asphalt shingle roof product, how important is the warranty? (Rating from 1 to 5 with 1 being of little importance and 5 being of extreme importance)

57.9% selected 5

25% selected 4

12% selected 3

2.9% selected 2

2.2% selected 1

Because re-roofing a home with asphalt shingles can be expensive, what is the minimum number of years of useful life you expect to get before you need to re-roof again?

37.6% said 25 years

34.3% said 20 years

15.1% said 30-plus years

9.9% said 15 years

1.8% said 10 years

1.2% said they didn't know

When you consider purchasing an asphalt shingle roof product, how important is the brand name? (Rating from 1 to 5 with 1 being of little importance and 5 being extremely important)

31.1% selected 4

27.9% selected 3

24.8% selected 5

8.4% selected 1

7.8% selected 2

Do you keep all warranty information about all products you purchase in a safe place so you can reference it in the future?

82.1% said Yes

15.3% said No

2.6% said they didn't know

For classification purposes only please answer the next two questions: What is your sex:

87.8% percent were male

11.3 percent were female

0.9% preferred not to disclose their sex

What is your age?

37.9% were between 56-65

35.8% were between 66-75

10.8% were between 46-55

10.4% were 76 or older

4.3% were 36-45

0.9% were 26-35

WHAT DOES THE DATA SAY?

I'm not a statistician. In fact, I didn't do so well in that math class back in college.

But looking at the data I'm fairly certain it's safe to say that a majority of homeowners who completed the survey expect their roofs to look good and be leak-free for twenty years or more.

A vast majority feel the warranty is important.

I feel you can then extrapolate the data to say that a huge majority of homeowners would be very unhappy if they started to experience severe degradation of their shingles after just ten years or so.

More Warranty Information

Let's take a look at a few of the warranty programs before they change. Over the past few years asphalt shingle warranties seem to change more frequently than the weather in Cincinnati, Ohio!

As I stated earlier, based on the evidence I've compiled while studying this roofing issue I pose this question: Do the marketing teams at most of the shingle manufacturers have as much or possibly more input on the warranties rather than the engineers in charge of making the shingles?

If you want to compare the warranties of the major asphalt shingle manufacturers, the place to start is the ARMA website:

http://www.asphaltroofing.org/

With minimal effort, you'll soon discover a list of residential manufacturers.

GAF stands out to me because for most of my career I used their products. The wholesale company in Cincinnati, OH that I purchased products from featured GAF shingles.

I had GAF shingles on my Queen Anne Victorian home in Cincinnati. Those were the shingles that still looked great after twenty-two years. GAF claims to be North America's largest roofing manufacturer, so I decided to look at their warranty.

I visited the GAF website while compiling this book and discovered a very informative page that compared their different warranties. To keep things simple, they had a Good, Better, and Best system.

The first thing that jumps out at me, but you might gloss over it, was the all-important phrase: Material Defect Coverage.

No matter how hard I tried, I couldn't find anywhere in GAF's warranty documentation what constitutes a material defect. Common sense dictates that if you want to file a valid warranty claim, you would have to prove to GAF that the shingles on your house have a 'material defect'.

I did further research on this, but let's continue to explore some of the interesting conditions on the warranty page.

Rather than get hung up on the warranty periods that range from 25 years to lifetime, let's focus on one of the footnotes. At the time of me writing this book here's what it said at the GAF website:

> "The word "Lifetime" means as long as the original individual owner of a single-family-detached residence (or the second owner in certain circumstances) owns the property where the shingles are installed. For owners/structures (e.g. a church) not meeting above criteria, Lifetime coverage is not applicable. See limited warranty for complete coverage and restrictions."

You'll discover similar wording as you read warranties and the referenced documents called out in some of the warranties of many of the other asphalt shingle manufacturers.

That wording should start a blinding blue and red LED light bar blinking behind you.

What's different about the roof at your local church when compared to your home? Both could have the same slope, the same compass orientation and both could have the GAF shingles applied by the same roofer using the same tools. In fact, your house could be next door to the church.

Imagine both roofs were installed the same day using the same exact GAF shingles from the same manufacturing run at the factory. Shouldn't the shingles last the same amount of time on both roofs?

The answer is yes.

But you get a lifetime warranty if you stay in your home and the church gets squat.

How can that be logical?

This nuance started to make sense to me once I thought about housing data provided by the National Association of Realtors (NAR) and the National Association of Home Builders (NAHB).

Both of these organizations spend vast amounts of money on surveys gathering data to discover how long the average person lives in their home. Both prestigious national associations have data that comes to just about the same conclusion.

When I contacted Adam DeSanctis, the media contact for the NAR, he got back to me within hours with this response:

> *Hi Tim,*
>
> *Thanks for reaching out.*
>
> *The U.S. Census Bureau tracks the homeownership rate and has data on the average age of homeownership. I'm not familiar with any figures on the average length of homeownership.*
>
> *In our annual Profile of Home Buyers and Sellers, we do track the median tenure in home. Over time, this number has been around 8 years. This past year it was 9; 10 in 2014. 10 years was the all-time high last year – which reflects that homeowners were staying in their homes a little bit longer to build equity lost since the downturn.*
>
> *Hope this helps!*
>
> *Adam DeSanctis | Economic Issues Media Manager, Media Communications*
>
> *National Association of Realtors® | 500 New Jersey Ave., NW, Washington, D.C. 20001*

Eight to ten years is the average length of time for home ownership. Do you find that interesting? I do.

TESTING FOR MANUFACTURING DEFECTS

Try as I may, I've not been able to discover on any of the asphalt shingle manufacturers' websites or in their written documentation a crisp definition of *manufacturing defect*.

To prove you have one, you need to look at an objective description of a shingle that is without defects. One would think that if you then have a shingle in your possession that doesn't have all the qualities and characteristics outlined in the objective description, then you have a product with a manufacturing defect.

If you talk to the management folks at the asphalt shingle manufacturers, my guess is they'll point to the ASTM standards as this baseline objective description. If you look at the specifications and descriptions of just about any asphalt shingle you've bought or are thinking of buying, you'll see one or more ASTM standards that the shingle meets or exceeds.

WHAT IS THE ASTM?

ASTM is an acronym that stands for the American Society for Testing and Materials. You can learn all the details about them at their website About section: http://www.astm.org/

At their website here's what they say about their organization:

> "ASTM International is a globally recognized leader in the development and delivery of voluntary consensus standards. Today, over 12,000 ASTM standards are used around the world to improve product quality, enhance health and safety, strengthen market access and trade, and build consumer confidence."

That might be confusing to you at first blush, but six words jumped out at me:

voluntary consensus standards

build consumer confidence

What does that mean to you?

For me to get a grasp on this, I reached out to the head ASTM public relations person, Erin Brennan. I called her on the phone and left a voice mail asking how an ASTM standard gets created and who's responsible for authoring the standard.

Erin responded in less than two hours starting an email discussion. Her first email was text copied from the FAQ page of their website. It was very helpful.

The first thing that happens is anyone, that could mean a company or an industry, submits a request to the ASTM for the new standard. The ASTM staff then researches the idea and makes an assessment to see if there is interest in the field for this new standard.

The ASTM does not determine which standards should be developed - their technical committees do that work.

I then sent a follow up email to Erin with this text:

> *"You say in your reply:*
>
> *How are ASTM standards developed?*
>
> *Standards development work begins when members of an ASTM technical committee identify a need or other interested parties approach the committee (see answer above).*
>
> *I couldn't see in the answer above how someone gets on the ASTM technical committee.*
>
> *In other words, is the Task Group that prepares the draft of a proposed standard made up of individuals who work for the companies whose products will be tested using the new ASTM standard?*
>
> *Thanks if you can shed light on this."*

Erin replied:

> *"Tim,*
>
> *Here is the specific answer, anyone can become a member of an ASTM committee. Committees are a balance of producers, users, consumers and general interest parties as stated below. Individuals like you mention may be a part of a committee if they choose to be and want to be part of the process.*
>
> *Who develops ASTM standards?*
>
> *ASTM has over 30,000 volunteer members from more than 140 countries around the world who are producers, users, consumers and general interest parties. These members write ASTM standards through*

their service on one or more of our 140-plus technical committees. It is these members who decide which standards development activities to pursue. Anyone interested in the field covered by a committee's scope is eligible to become a committee member.

For specific information on the ins and outs of the voting and balloting process, see http://www.astm.org/COMMIT/Regs.pdf

Voting Privileges—Every ASTM member is entitled to vote on all Society Review items as well as on each ballot of a main committee and subcommittee to which the member belongs. All negatives and comments received from all ballot returns, including those from non-official voting members, shall be considered in accordance with these regulations."

Yes, I realize that's all pretty technical, but did you pull out of Erin's answers very important key information?

Anyone can become a member of an ASTM committee. The asphalt shingle manufacturers can all sit on the committee that develops the standard to test shingles.

The committee assists in creating the ASTM standard.

Has that sunk in yet? Have you processed what that means? Do you remember the first ASTM language we looked at, the one that mentions "voluntary consensus standards"?

LOWEST COMMON DENOMINATOR

I've not sat on an ASTM committee that's working to develop a standard and my guess is a vast majority of people have not.

But my understanding of what's in play is that those sitting on the committee creating the standard come to a consensus decision of what the standard should be.

It would make sense that the standard would be a set of minimum conditions that all of the members on the committee could achieve with their product that's being tested. In fact, it might make sense to put the bar low enough so that any product being tested might exceed the standard by some generous percentage.

The best analogy I can offer up to describe this method would be a fox guarding the henhouse. Perhaps you can come up with a better one.

CATCH 22

I've done expert witness testimony in lawsuits involving building issues for over fifteen years. I discovered early on that if you want to win lawsuits you point to some standard that's very objective and has a crisp description of how something should be or should have been done.

In my past expert-testimony work, I leaned heavily on the building code that was in force at the time the home was built that was in the center of the lawsuit.

Let's assume your roof goes bad and you decide to file a lawsuit against the manufacturer because they dodge you and won't pay out on what appears to you to be a manufacturing defect.

If you have a good attorney and expert on your side, my guess is they'll go look at the ASTM standards to see if the shingle on your home met the standard.

How would you feel if you discovered that the test that needs to be performed to determine if a shingle is defective can only be done within a short amount of time after it comes off the factory floor?

If a standard was written that way, that would make it impossible for you to ever claim there was a manufacturing defect because the test can't produce accurate results if the shingle's been up on your roof for one, five, or ten years.

ASTM D3462

If you do some research you'll quickly discover an ASTM standard used by the asphalt roofing manufacturers. It's ASTM D3462 - Standard Specification for Asphalt Shingles Made from Glass Felt and Surfaced with Mineral Granules

That's a fancy description for the shingles that are on your home. If you visit the ASTM website and look at the simple page that describes this standard you'll discover some troubling language. At least I found it troubling.

Just below the Abstract of the standard, you'll see the first point:

1. Scope

1.1 This specification covers asphalt roofing in shingle form, composed of glass felt or felts impregnated and coated on both sides with asphalt, and surfaced on the weather side with mineral granules. This specification is designed for the evaluation of products as manufactured. The test methods, physical requirements, and minimum masses are to be measured immediately after packaging or at a reasonable time, as agreed upon between buyer and seller, after manufacture and before installation. Physical and performance requirements after application and during in-service use of the products described herein are beyond the scope of this material specification.

Did you understand that? It means that if you want to see if the shingle meets the standard you need to test it "immediately after packaging or at a reasonable time as agreed upon between the buyer and seller, after manufacture and before installation."

The last sentence is the one that should have you fuming. It means that once the shingles are on your home, even for a day, the "performance requirements" are "beyond the scope of this material specification".

In layman's terms that means you can't prove legally that your shingles have a manufacturing defect. PERIOD.

VENTILATION

I wanted to inject another fact into the mix before we move on. It's about roof and attic ventilation.

If your asphalt shingle roof has gone bad and a company representative who visits your home tries to tell you the shingles failed because of inadequate ventilation, you might want to challenge them. In the 1970s attic and roof ventilation technology started to change. As houses were better insulated and the use of plastic vapor barriers started to expand, it became important to get the water vapor that floated up into attics back out to the atmosphere.

Older homes built prior to World War II were generally drafty and water vapor would pass through to the outside air before it drifted up to the attic of a home. What's more, the houses were so drafty that lower-humidity air would mix with the indoor air lowering its overall relative humidity.

These same homes didn't have any modern attic or roof ventilation, yet as I've shown you the older shingles didn't crumble and fall apart. In other words, state-of-the-art roof ventilation was not necessary to prevent shingles of old from falling apart.

HEAT CONTROL

We've already discussed how higher roof temperatures accelerate the oxidation chemical reaction of shingles. You might hear shingle manufacturers or their representatives tell you that the lack of adequate ventilation can cause the shingles to get too hot leading to premature shingle failure.

Once again, if that's the case, then why didn't the roofs of old fail? Older homes simply didn't have continuous soffit and ridge vents. Most homes had tiny gable vents at the two ends of the house.What's more, don't think for a moment that adequate ventilation will significantly lower the temperature of the asphalt shingles on your roof at high noon on a summer's day. You could have tens of thousands of cubic feet of air blowing through your attic and the actual temperature of the asphalt in your shingles will be nearly the same with no air moving through the attic.

WHAT NOW TIM?

You may have an asphalt shingle roof that needs to be replaced.

You may be getting ready to build a home and want to know what kind of roofing material has the best chance of lasting like the shingles of old.

Perhaps you just put on a new asphalt shingle roof in the past five years and want to know if you're doomed.

I've got great news for you.

CHAPTER ELEVEN
THE CAVALRY IS COMING

When I was up on my very hot roof removing shingles in June of 2015, I was angry. The crumbling shingles fell apart in my own hands. I was stunned at the degree of deterioration.

I was determined to put a roof over my family's head that would not fail and I fully intended to get to the bottom of what was going on after I solved my immediate roof issue.

There are quite a few alternative products you can select when roofing a home. If you're about to build a new home or need to re-roof your home, you've got choices. Among them are:

- wood shakes
- real slate
- clay tile
- concrete tile
- metal roofing
- synthetic slate
- rubber

I'm sure there could be other niche products, but the list above contains mainstream products. Each of them has their pros and cons. Some require maintenance, some require extra support because of the weight, and some require very skilled installation.

APPEARANCE CAN BE IMPORTANT

Not all products look good on a particular home. Listen to a panel discussion of seasoned architects and my guess is you'll soon discover that the texture, color and appearance of roofing material factors in to how you feel about the overall appearance of a home. In my case, my house sits down in a hole and when you drive down my driveway all you see is the roof of my home.

For this reason, my wife and I decided we'd really like to use a product that had great curb appeal and would complement the architectural style of our home. The

Here's a photo of my current home in New Hampshire. My garage roof would make a great place for a billboard.

product also had to be one that would last for many decades.

We decided to use a virgin polymer synthetic slate. It's made by DaVinci Roofscapes. Just about every person that comes to our house the first time mentions the roof as soon as they see us. It's that good looking.

What you'll discover if you decide to abandon asphalt shingles as I did is that just about every option is quite expensive. That's a deal breaker for most people and it's understandable.

As I wrote this book, I made two significant discoveries. If you can only afford asphalt shingles, I've got very good news for you.

THE MAGIC ELIXIR

You've heard the old saying "Don't throw the baby out with the bathwater.", haven't you?

I think it applies in this case.

The good news is there's a shingle that's made with a unique ingredient that's blended into the asphalt. If you're about to purchase asphalt shingles for your home, this is a shingle you might want to consider.

The fancy name for this ingredient is styrene butadiene styrene or SBS. This chemical polymer adds interesting and beneficial characteristics when it's blended with the hot asphalt used to make shingles.

The SBS polymer was first introduced to asphalt shingles in 1986 by the Malarkey Roofing Company. They put it in a special shingle line made for Alaskan roofers so they could install shingles when the outdoor temperature dropped to 0 F. If you try to install regular shingles in extreme cold weather they'll often crack.

PURE ASPHALT = LESS OXIDATION

If you remember from earlier in our journey we discovered manufacturers of old pre-aged the asphalt to raise the softening point from 120 F up to around 200 F so it wouldn't flow off your roof on a hot summer's day.

They blew oxygen into the pure asphalt from the oil refinery trying to get some of the asphalt molecules to cross-link with one another.

The pre-aging, or oxidation, process robs the asphalt of some of its useful life and makes it stiffer.

Guess What?

When you introduce the SBS polymer into asphalt and do it right, you can raise the softening point of the asphalt up to 200 F, or slightly above, without the need to oxidize or pre-age it. That translates to a longer life for your asphalt shingles.

Super Sticky

The SBS has an additional very positive quality in that it's a super adhesive. If you purchase shingles that contain this polymer it will undoubtedly help in keeping the ceramic colored-stone granules on the shingles for a longer time. As you already know, UV light supercharges asphalt oxidation so it's vital the granules stay attached to your shingles.

The polymer also helps with thermal cycling recovery. This means each day as the shingles heat up and cool down they stay flexible through many more cycles. Instead of the shingles losing more granules and curling up like a crispy potato chip, the shingles stay flat, flexible and flawless for much longer than asphalt shingles that don't contain this extraordinary ingredient.

Another benefit of the SBS polymer is it helps to make shingles more resistant to hail damage. The added elasticity of the polymer helps ensure the all-important ceramic granules stay in place when they're pounded by pieces of hail.

The asphalt paving industry also uses this SBS polymer to help keep asphalt roads in better shape for longer periods of time.

Who Makes Shingles That Contain SBS?

As of the spring of 2017 the following is a list of companies that I could locate that made asphalt shingles that contain the SBS polymer. When you look at the list below, don't assume that *each shingle product* made by the manufacturer has this important ingredient. Realize that manufacturers offer different product lines that vary in look, composition and price.

It's possible all shingles have some amount of SBS polymer in them, but they may not contain enough of it to impart the all-important longer-life characteristics it can offer. Some industry experts claim that the asphalt brew should have an SBS content of eight to twelve percent. I wish you the best of luck should you try to go on a quest asking a particular manufacturer how much SBS polymer they put in their asphalt. My guess is they'll not share that information with you.

I feel if a manufacturer is touting on their website that a particular line of shingles has the SBS polymer, they're telegraphing to you they feel they may be putting in enough to make a difference.

When you visit the websites of the following manufacturers, you must pay close attention and look for descriptive text that convinces you they're using the SBS polymer. After an exhaustive search, here's the list I was able to compile of manufacturers that say they use SBS polymer in some of their shingles:

- Atlas Roofing Corporation
- Certainteed
- GAF
- Malarkey Roofing Products

Why Don't All Shingles Have SBS?

Here's a fascinating factoid. The polymer doesn't add significant cost to the manufacturing process because just a small percentage is added, by volume, to the asphalt at the shingle plant. Even if it did add significant cost, my guess is there's a certain percentage of homeowners who would purchase it based on the results of my warranty survey.

That should cause you to wonder, "Why don't all the manufacturers use the SBS polymer?"

That's a great question if I don't say so myself. If you price asphalt shingles that contain the SBS polymer, you'll discover they cost more than those that don't have this ingredient. A manufacturer who has chosen not to use SBS may argue they just want to offer the consumer an affordable alternative.

Don't Forget

But before you get completely amazed by the wonders of the SBS polymer, and I agree it's a wonderful additive, realize that prior to 1986 shingles were made without it that lasted thirty or more years. In other words, shingles don't require this extra chemical to hold onto the colored granules and not curl up for decades and decades.

Remember my friend Russ's shingles? They're still laying flat and have many of the granules on them, yet they were made in 1965 long before SBS polymer was a glimmer in the eye of the chemists and management team of Malarkey Roofing Products.

This should be another point you stuff in your backpack. You may reach a decision earlier than others about there being sufficient circumstantial evidence beyond a reasonable doubt that some asphalt shingles are being engineered to fail long before they should.

Saving Your New, Newer or Older Roof

Did you just put a new asphalt shingle roof on your home before reading this book? Are you wringing your hands wondering if you wasted your money? Is your asphalt shingle roof less than seven years old?

Do you have an older asphalt shingle roof that's still in very good condition?

Are you about to purchase new shingles and you're concerned that they could fail sooner than later for any number of reasons?

Are you going to purchase shingles with the SBS polymer and then hope that it works? Remember, hope is the emotion of last resort. You hope for things you can't control.

How would you like to be able to put something on your roof that would magically allow new asphalt shingles you buy today to perform like the shingles I used to put on all those many years ago?

I'm talking about having an asphalt shingle roof that could last for multiple decades. Imagine having a roof that could last as long as my friend Russ in southern California or like the Inselbric product on all the buildings around the

USA?

I've got very good news for you, and I'm afraid it's going to be very bad news for the sales managers at all the roofing manufacturers.

THE 8-FOOT-WIDE STRIP

The day after Christmas 2015 I was fortunate to see a roof near my home that holds clear-cut evidence that you can slow the oxidation of the asphalt in your new or newer shingles. I saw this roof about two months after finishing the installation of the roof on my own home.

Remember, oxidation is what causes the ceramic granules to fall off and then causes the shingles to curl. You want to slow, or stop, this oxidation.

THE COPPER-ROOFED CUPOLA

Look at the striking photo below and see if you can tell how simple it is to extend the life of your asphalt shingle roof. You're looking at a simple chemical reaction where copper washing off the cupola roof is bonding to the asphalt in place of oxygen that's in the air.

On the day after Christmas in 2015, I was walking out the door of a restaurant in Tilton, New Hampshire and I looked across the street to the vacant old post office building. Instantly I saw how copper could help to extend the life of your asphalt shingle roof. The shingles that were in good condition are proof of a simple chemical reaction where copper washing off the cupola roof is bonding to the asphalt in place of oxygen that's in the air.

Some of the UV rays of the sun are so powerful, they split off copper ions from the solid copper. Each time it rains, these copper ions are gently transported down across the asphalt shingles.

Based on what you're observing in the photo there's absolutely no doubt the copper allows the asphalt to retain much or most of its flexibility. The copper ions attach to the asphalt molecules where the oxygen would normally connect. However, the copper ions don't promote the cross-linking of the asphalt molecules to one another.

Because there's little cross-linking occurring, the asphalt retains its flexibility allowing it to hold onto the ceramic granules. The shingles also exhibit no curling, except for those in the photo that are farthest away from the copper roof on the cupola.

Curling happens because the asphalt has lost its flexibility due to too much cross-linking.

This is a striking photo of the roof of the vacant Tilton, New Hampshire Post Office. Note the 8-foot-wide strip of shingles that are in almost perfect condition below the cupola with the copper roof.

Install Copper ASAP

If you've just installed an asphalt shingle roof, or have one that's less than seven years old, all you need to do is put copper strips across the top of your shingles. I'd suggest you have a minimum of one square foot of exposed copper for every 50 square feet of asphalt shingle below the exposed copper.

The average roof usually has 25 feet, or less, of distance from the peak of the roof down to the gutter or eave edge. If this is the case, then you just need a 6-inch strip of copper up at the peak of the roof.

INSTALL A 12-INCH-WIDE RIDGE STRIP

Perhaps the easiest way to achieve this is to apply a 12-inch-wide strip of copper over the ridge at the peak of your roof. Six inches of the copper will now be exposed on each side of the roof.

If you have a hip roof, you need to install the copper strip up each hip where the cap shingles would normally be.

If you have ridge vent on your roof, then just lay the copper strip on top of this instead of the normal cap shingles. This will save you the cost of the cap shingles which can be significant.

If you're trying to protect a newer roof, then just nail the copper over the top of the existing cap shingles.

REGULAR RAINFALL

The reason the copper protected the shingles in the photo of the old post office in Tilton, NH is because for eight months out of the year there's regular rainfall that distributes the copper ions to the asphalt.

If you live west of the Great Plains in the USA, except for the Pacific Northwest, you usually don't get nearly the annual rainfall we get east of the Great Plains. In fact, in many places there are long dry periods where there's little rain.

I don't feel you can imitate Mother Nature's rainfall with a garden hose. Based on what I observed on that post office roof in Tilton, NH, I feel the gentle and periodic rainfall we get in New Hampshire slowly delivers the copper ions to the shingles.

If you try to get up on your roof and hose down the copper strip at the ridge you may add too much water and wash all the copper ions off the roof.

Because of this, you'll need to do something else in addition to installing the copper strips. You'll need to periodically spray your roof with a liquid solution that contains copper ions.

Copper Sulfate For Dry Climates

In my opinion the best way to do this is by dissolving inexpensive copper sulfate crystals in hot tap water from a sink. At room temperature you should be able to get 21.95 grams of copper sulfate crystals to dissolve in 100 grams of water so long as you use hot water and you stir the crystals until they dissolve.

It might be easier for you to work in gallons of water and pounds of copper sulfate crystals. To get the highest amount of copper into a gallon of water, mix 1.8 pounds of copper sulfate. It dissolves quite rapidly in hot water.

Apply this solution to the shingles so they get saturated, but not so much that the solution pours off your roof. I'd apply this solution at least once a month in the dry season if you want to significantly increase the lifespan of your asphalt shingles.

As the solution dries, the water is liberated into the atmosphere and the copper chemically bonds to the ends of the asphalt molecules broken apart by the UV rays of the sun. This prevents the cross-linking that makes the asphalt stiff and brittle.

If your roof water feeds a cistern from which you draw drinking water, be sure you routinely test your water to ensure the water you drink has safe levels of copper.

Copper Prevents Black Algae Stains

This same copper, whether it's the solid-copper strips or the copper solution you spray, will prevent the black stains caused by the roof algae I discussed earlier in the book. The algae doesn't like the taste of the copper and it travels to another location to feast.

You'll pay several hundred dollars (2017 pricing) to have solid copper strips installed on the average roof, but it could end up saving you thousands and thousands of dollars by extending the life of your asphalt shingles by ten, twenty or possibly thirty years!

Purchasing Copper Strips and Copper Sulfate

There are many sources for the copper products. I've seen rolls of copper at my local lumberyard and at the giant home centers.

Copper sulfate is readily available online and at agricultural stores you might have out in the country near rural areas.

When I made my discovery about the copper / asphalt chemical reaction I tried to see if it was patentable. After talking with three different skilled patent attorneys I was told I could get a design patent, but that's an easy thing to work around.

Full Disclosure

My discovery, unfortunately, was an *"undiscovered benefit"* of a previous patent. Other inventors years ago had patented the use of copper strips up on roofs for any number of other reasons. It turns out that other inventors never thought of how copper could interact with the asphalt molecules.

The reason I discovered it is because the owner of the Tilton, NH Post Office building allowed the roof to deteriorate to such a degree that it became obvious. Many other building owners would have replaced the roof many years before and not given it much thought as to why the shingles under the cupola were not as worn.

The bottom line is that I was unable to obtain a patent for my chemical discovery. Because I could not get a patent, I decided to partner up with a great company near me to sell the exact copper strip that would work perfectly for your roof. I wanted to make sure you'd get the exact protection you needed for the least amount of money.

Remember, you can purchase copper from many other sources. You don't need to buy it from me and that's not why I wrote this book. As with any purchase, just do your due diligence and make sure you're purchasing the best copper that will work.

If you decide to purchase the copper strip I'm selling, I include the exact nails you need to keep the copper on the roof ridge where it belongs. After you check other sources for copper roof strips, you may want to look at what I'm offering. Go to:

http://go.askthebuilder.com/copperstrips

If you're going to type that URL into a device, do not put www in front of the word go.

Be sure when you buy your copper you install it with copper or stainless-steel nails. If you use aluminum or galvanized roofing nails, you'll get a galvanic reaction and a non-copper nail may corrode in a short amount of time. If this happens, your copper strip will fly off your roof on the next windy day.

I'd recommend you put the copper strips on your roof no matter what shingles you buy. The reason is simple. It's an insurance policy that can save you many thousands of dollars. The best part is the copper can be reused by the next homeowner decades from now.

Can you imagine what it might cost to re-roof your house in fifteen years? The price may take your breath away. Don't take a chance *hoping* your next asphalt roof will last.

You know that copper will protect your investment.

THE FINAL STRUGGLE

You now know how to put a roof over your head that's going to last decades. But if you're like most, you'll not be doing any of the work yourself.

Most people have no clue how to do roofing work, they don't own the equipment and they're afraid of heights.

You'll need to hire someone, but how will you know you won't get taken?

Follow me please.

CHAPTER TWELVE
HIRING A PRO ROOFER

I'd like to think I was a real professional when I was still in the field actively building and remodeling. I was chosen as one of the Big 50* remodelers in the USA in 1993 by *Remodeling* magazine and I leveraged that award to launch my Ask the Builder career.

I know I could have done much better with respect to business practices and handling customers, but when it came to my work, I always strived to do the absolute best job possible. Several of my sub-contractor friends remind me to this day that I was a perfectionist on the job site.

With that background, I believe I can help you find the best possible person in your community to do your roofing work. I've been counseling homeowners for over twenty years how to locate the pros. It will require some work on your part, but it will be well worth it.

A SMALL GROUP

If you ask ten different people what qualities make a tradesman a professional,

I surmise you'd get at least six different answers. It's somewhat subjective.

One of the first qualities, in my opinion, a professional exudes is he treats his work as a vocation, not a job. How can you identify this characteristic? It's not easy, but there are indirect ways to do it.

Realize that professionals, I mean real ones, represent a very tiny percentage when you put all the same tradesmen in a room. It's the same in any vertical. There are superbly talented certified public accountants (CPAs), there are good ones, there are ones that just passed the rigorous exams and then there are the really bad CPAs.

You know this to be the case in just about any profession or with people in life. Roofers are no different. Here's how I'd locate the best roofer, or a group of them, in your town if I came to visit you.

I'd first locate the businesses that sell roofing products. I'd avoid the giant chain big box stores. If you live in a bigger city, there are invisible businesses that you've never heard of that sell products to professionals.

These are distributorships for some of the bigger or medium-sized brands. In smaller towns you'll probably discover the traditional lumber yard is where you'll find roofing products. That's the way it is here in central New Hampshire where I live.

Pros Know How to Make a Fair Profit

Professionals know that two things eat into profits faster than rain melts soft snow. The first is a service call due to a failed product. If a contractor has to go back to fix something because a product failed, not the installation of the product, it really sets him back financially.

The second indirect issue is the bad feelings the service call creates with the customer. The last thing a professional wants is a customer to have a loss of faith in his, the contractor's, abilities.

For this reason, most professionals only purchase the absolute best products so they don't fail. Yes, it's possible for a freak problem but more often than not great products perform well for many years.

The invisible businesses that sell to roofers almost always stock these great products. You don't always find them at the big box retailers.

Visit And Ask Questions

To find the pro, you need to be proactive. Forget about reading the online reviews at some of the websites that help you try to find a pro. You do realize some of the reviews might not be honest, don't you?

You need to get into your car and drive to these roofing suppliers or lumberyards that sell varied roofing supplies. Arrive mid morning or mid-afternoon. Professionals are almost always on the job site at this time of day. They'll be at the businesses getting materials early in the day, at lunch, or at the end of the day.

When you show up at the slower periods, you should be able to have a conversation with the general manager or the business owner. Don't be afraid to ask for this person.

Tell them I sent you.

Here are the four questions you want to ask them:

- Can you give me the names of roofers who have been buying from you for over fifteen years?
- Who are the roofers that always buy the best products you sell?
- Who are the roofers that pay their bills before they're due so they get the 2-percent discount?
- What's the short list of roofers you'd get bids from to work on your own home?

You want a roofer that's stood the test of time in business. Fifteen years is a decent amount of time.

You want a roofer that buys the best products. I've already said why.

You want a roofer that's a good businessman and understands how to harvest free money. He can then reinvest this money in his business. Contractors can get this free money by paying their bills early. Many businesses reward early payment with a cash discount.

When I was still building, it was not uncommon for me to realize thousands of extra dollars of profit by paying my invoices early. I used this money to reward my employees, buy the best tools and create a cushion for tough times.

The general managers and owners of these businesses are no fools. They know who the best roofers are. Who do you think they want working on their own homes? They want the best, of course!

If you just take the time to do this simple exercise and have a talk with the right people, you're going to find the best tradespeople in your town. You're also going to see some great products at this business you've never seen before.

GETTING FREE BIDS

I also have a relationship with a website called HomeAdvisor.com. This is a website where contractors purchase the contact information of homeowners like you.

You've seen websites where you can get free quotes from numerous contractors. You fill out a form and soon you get phone calls from local contractors who want your business.

HomeAdvisor is one of these websites that offers this free service to you. Websites like www.AsktheBuilder.com that have links to HomeAdvisor get a small commission for brokering the contact. It's very similar to how real estate agents make their living. They broker a deal between a buyer and a seller.

If you want free bids from local roofers that are connected to HomeAdvisor. com, then click the following link or enter it into your browser. If you fill out the form, I'll get a small commission from HomeAdvisor. It costs you nothing to fill out the form.

http://go.askthebuilder.com/freeroofingbids

Do not put the www in front of the word go.

It's not going to be a waste of time for you to visit your local businesses or to get free bids from local roofing contractors.

CHAPTER THIRTEEN
JOURNEY'S END

Our journey's ended.

You may have mixed emotions. I know I do.

Years ago I was a licensed real estate broker in the state of Ohio. Every three years I was required to take thirty hours of continuing education to maintain my license. One of the required courses in each three-year cycle was Ethics.

You'd think if you took the class one time, you'd not have to take it again. But as time passed I could see why it was so important. Things can change in a person's life and pressure can force the individual to make an unethical decision that years before he/she would have avoided.

Keep in mind you can be engaged in legal activity each day in your life, but you can be very unethical at the same time.

Ethics are completely different than law. That's why they're two different words.

I'm convinced in my own heart that many of the asphalt shingle manufacturers know how to make a product that lasts and lasts. A certain percentage of the population desires this kind of product.

The stories, photos, survey results, and facts I've presented to you are sobering.

For decades long-lasting shingles covered homes and businesses, but the data I collected speaks volumes that many homeowners like you seem to have a product that's not performing as it should.

Warranty Expectations

The average consumer equates the length of a warranty to how long a product will last before it fails. Usually the warranty even states that. Surely you've seen language in a warranty that may state, "We warrant this product will be free of defects for XX years."

Once you go past the warranty period, it's expected the product will start to fail or break down.

Perhaps you want to purchase a shingle that's made with the special SBS polymer and it's not offered in your city or town. Did you know you can buy these from a distant distributor and he'll arrange to have them shipped to your local lumber yard? The shipping and local delivery fee may be well worth it to have shingles that can last for decades.

If you don't want to do that and you have no idea if the shingles you're buying will last, then maybe you'll just decide to put copper strips along the top of your roof to protect your investment.

Realize that you do have options. If you decide to not even take a chance with asphalt shingles in the future, just be sure you read all of the installation instructions provided by the manufacturer before you hire the roofer to install whatever you buy. You want to quiz the roofer to make sure he understands how to work with the non-asphalt product.

Please Join My Virtual Family

I'd love for you to become part of my Ask the Builder family. We can stay in touch each week when you subscribe to my free newsletter.

Go to http://www.AsktheBuilder.com now and subscribe to my FREE newsletter. As a subscriber you'll receive regular updates about anything that may change with respect to asphalt shingles.

You'll also receive notifications of new book projects I'm working on as well as other products that can help you save time and money around your home.

I've already outlined the next book and if the email I receive every week is any clue, it should be of great help to you.

Amazon Reviews

If you purchased this book on www.amazon.com, I'd sincerely appreciate it if you'd go back and leave an honest review. Help other homeowners so they don't lose their life savings.

You and I are blessed to be able to share opinions and reviews online. Years ago it was nearly impossible for an author to publish honest reviews from normal folks like us. You've read great reviews and know how they've influenced your decisions to purchase something.

Please help guide others who might want to invest in the nuggets of information you discovered here.

I also ask that you consider visiting the website created just for this book. This website contains homeowner stories, photos and other information that may be of great interest to you:

http://www.RoofingRipoff.com

Please consider sharing your comments there about this book. If you have an asphalt shingle roof that's deteriorating, feel free to share your story and pictures at the website.

Tim Carter
Founder - http://www.AsktheBuilder.com

RESOURCES

The following is a list of resources that were used to compile the information in this book.

J. L. Strahan, Technical Director - Asphalt Roofing Industry Bureau. "Manufacture, Selection, and Application of Asphalt Roofing and Siding Products" Fourth Edition, 1952

Malarkey, Greg. "The History of Asphalt Shingles" *Interface* April 2001 Pages 5-9

ARMA - http://www.asphaltroofing.org/

Blowing Asphalt - http://www.e-asfalto.com/ingles/oxidador/index.htm

Inselbric Advertisement *Life* May 17, 1954

John Davis. "Modified Asphalt Strengthens Roofing Shingles" *Asphalt* http://asphaltmagazine.com/modified-asphalt-strengthens-roofing-shingles/

American Society of Testing Materials - https://www.astm.org/

Atlas Roofing Corporation: http://www.atlasroofing.com/

Building Products of Canada: http://www.bpcan.com/

Certainteed Roofing: https://www.certainteed.com/

GAF: http://www.gaf.com/

Henry Company: http://www.henry.com/

IKO Production, Inc.: https://www.iko.com/

Malarkey Roofing Products: https://malarkeyroofing.com/

Owens Corning: https://www.owenscorning.com/roofing

PABCO Roofing Products: http://www.pabcoroofing.com/

Polyglass USA, Inc.: http://www.polyglass.com/

Siplast Incorporated: http://www.siplast.com/

TAMKO Building Products, Inc.: https://www.tamko.com/

Tarco: http://www.tarcoroofing.com/

W.R. Grace & Co.: https://grace.com/en-us

Copper Development Association: https://www.copper.org/

www.ingramcontent.com/pod-product-compliance
Lightning Source LLC
Chambersburg PA
CBHW040513290326

41930CB00035B/6